Think Like a Rich Chick! And Make Money Online.

The Step-By-Step Guide to Creating a Multiple 6-Figure Income, Doing What You Love!

Book 3 in the Think Like a Rich Chick series.

International Amazon Best-Selling Author Kat Loterzo

Published by: Katrina Loterzo Pty Ltd
Edited by: Deanna Shanti – Shanti Publishing

Cover Designed by: Kyle Hoobin – Milk Jug Media

www.katloterzo.com

ISBN: 978-0994584700

Each month I give away a different one of my books for free! Receive your free book and join my online community of KICKASS women entrepreneurs at:

www.katloterzo.com

For more kickass books for kickass women, including free downloads:

www.booksforkickasswomen.com

Contents

CHAPTER ONE - TO YOUR SUCCESS!

In 2007 I made a decision that was, over the next 3-5 years, to completely change my life and what I imagined might be possible. I had no idea that this somewhat 'off the cuff' move to begin a blog and thus broaden my offerings to my personal training clients would, within 6 years, lead me to running a multi-faceted online company generating over $50,000 per month and allowing me to work, live and play from anywhere in the world and completely on my terms.

In this book I'm going to share my story with you, as well my most successful strategies, tools and tricks (and a few that didn't work!) so that you too can create a business you love, make a difference in the world, and make great money to boot, but first - and most importantly of all - I want to tell you this:

Whatever you dream for yourself, is possible.

Whatever you believe you could, maybe, one day - if you're lucky! - create, you can.

But if you want to turn those one day hopes, dreams and fantasies into reality you need to make a choice, right now, that you WILL. Not that you 'might' or that you'll 'give it a crack', but that you will. And then start taking immediate action.

If there's one thing I really want this book to do for you is to teach you that it has nothing to do with the actual processes I've used to create a successful and continually growing online business and it has everything to do with the MINDSET I've had and that you need to persevere until you get there.

I've seen people follow every step of a strategic approach and bomb out completely because they don't believe enough to keep going when the going gets tough. Even the most 'perfect' plan means nothing if you don't keep on implementing.

On the other hand, I've seen people with little or no strategy, tactics, support or plan create incredible success because they simply refused to say die. The greatest determining factor of where you end up in business is your attitude and what you INSIST on creating.

So decide right now.

Join me in saying - and say it aloud, please! -

I make the commitment to create my dream business, and I will not stop until I get there.

I make a commitment to keep on keeping on, no matter how tough or frustrating it seems at times, and no matter what happens in my life.

I make a commitment to just move forward, even when I have no idea what comes next.

I make a commitment to CHOOSE to believe (and it is a choice). I choose to believe that if I refuse to fail, I can't. I choose to believe that if I insist on winning, I will.

And I choose to have faith. I have faith that I can get there, even though I'm not exactly sure right now where 'there' is! I have faith that my hard work will pay off. I have faith that I can make as much money as I like, and that I can do it completely on my terms and by sharing a message that matters.

I have faith that I can succeed at being me.

And I'm going to start now.

CHAPTER TWO – HOW I QUIT MY PERSONAL TRAINING BUSINESS AND CREATED A $50K+ PER MONTH ONLINE INCOME, DOING WHAT I LOVE

My business story is long, and it's still evolving. What I might tell you about it this week is probably greatly different to what I'd say next week or certainly a few months from now! Sometimes when I look back I forget just how hard I fought to get to where I am, and I have to remind myself of how much I've earned my success. But I also have to remind myself of what an incredible evolution it's been. Since joining the World Wide Web in 2007 I've gone from 'wanting to be a writer' to not only creating massive financial success but proving to myself that I can truly create my DREAMS.

In the below 3 posts, which are extracted from my blog, I share with you the exact process of how I created that success. This is a story not only of what I did, but of what is possible for any of us when we have the right mental attitude in place. I'm sharing it with you in the hopes that I can inspire you, no matter where you are now, to know that whatever you dream for yourself is possible and you CAN, and will, prevail if you just keep moving forward!

How I quit 1:1 personal training and created a $50K+ per month online business - Part 1

2007 was a big year for me. Looking back it was in many ways one of the best years of my life, as it was the year I began creating the business that has now led to me living my dream life and enjoying over 50k per month of online income, all from doing what I love.

But at the time? It kinda sucked, for the most part!

I was going through a lengthy and messy divorce, learning to be completely in charge of my own money and life. At the same time, I had ignored all my friends and family's dire warnings about timing and 'needing a proper break first' and had started a new relationship with the man who would later become my lifelong partner and father of my children.

At least on the career side of things, everything was going

well – my Personal Training business consumed my time and energy from 6am until 9pm on weekdays, with just enough breathing room in between clients for a killer workout and a short black coffee or 5 :) Now, 6 years into life as a Personal Trainer I was 'all over it' when it came to signing up new clients and getting them great results. The other trainers joked that my day was like a well-oiled procession chain – one in, one out. I booked myself back to back with up to 20 sessions in a day, and I was bringing home over 5 grand a week in exchange for my efforts.

Not bad for a girl who walked away from a potential and long-planned career as a lawyer to become a gym instructor at age 19!

Of course if you're a 1:1 trainer or coach yourself I don't have to tell you how relentless that life can be.

If you don't have enough clients it's stressful and worrying (as well as disheartening to spend time on free trials with tire kickers or people who don't respect your time) and if you DO have enough clients it's absolutely exhausting and you start to resent the feeling that you no longer control your day, let alone your life.

And as much as they money is GREAT in 1:1 – or can be – it requires that ongoing effort. As soon as you stop, the money stops as well. Not exactly the dream business, right?

For me, I already knew I couldn't keep going for much longer like this. Not only were the days much too long to sustain, but I was suffering severe insomnia (a 'good' night was 1-2 hours of sleep) since my marriage break-up, and I couldn't seem to shake it. My impressive income seemed to disappear as fast as it came in as I scheduled near-daily Shiatsu massage, Acupuncture, Network Chiropractic, Kinesiology, sessions with my Psychologist/GP who was helping me try to shake off the bulimia I'd reverted straight back to post-marriage ending, and basically anything else that I thought would help me either sleep or feel like I would ever again be able to smile.

Like a machine, I moved through my days eating a bare minimum of 'fuel' in between clients then collapsing into binge-eating oblivion at night.

As fast as the dollars rolled in my spirit and enjoyment of life faded into nothing.

And certainly a big part of how I felt despite my Personal Training business 'success' was due to the mess that was my personal life.

But an equally big part was the unshakeable reality that I did NOT want to stay bound to 1:1 forever.

A couple of things happened around that time that caused me to make a decision eventually leading me to where I am now – which is making waaaay more than double what I used to make on even my most chock-full PT weeks and in about 1/10th of the time. Plus – completely on my terms.

Dreaming of being a 6-figure trainer NOT just through 1:1

The first thing I did was I went to the annual fitness conference Filex, and attended a presentation on being a '6-figure trainer'. Well, I already was a '6-figure trainer' but this presentation was about leveraging your time and knowledge and creating income outside of just 1:1. I wasn't so interested in the idea of doing group sessions or boot camps but the concept of bringing in big money for doing corporate health presentations or perhaps running some kind of subscription based email and phone coaching program fascinated me.

It was my first insight into the concept of online marketing and selling.

I joined a coaching program with the presenter from that day, and started putting together flyers and packages to tempt my clients and their companies with ideas for ways to reach more people at once and create a higher hourly wage. I was able to book a few speaking gigs and it looked like maybe this was 'it', my way out of 1:1.

I was pumped! And more than ready to step into living my 'real' purpose and passion. If only I could fully figure out what that was :)

Around the same time one of my long-term clients started to question why I didn't have a website yet or at least a newsletter. I remember saying that I was going to have one soon, but at the same time thinking 'ugh, sounds like a lot of work'. I certainly had no idea just how powerful an online presence – even a basic and pretty ugly one – could be.

But my new business mentor had also been touting the benefits of having a client newsletter and so I decided to set one up. The added bonus was that I loved to write – in fact, I had studied Professional Writing & Editing briefly at University after I had halted my pursuit of a Law degree. I had no strategy or purpose for my newsletter other than to position me as more professional with my clients. Really I was just doing it because my coach said I should :)

My clients loved the newsletter and my fumbling attempts at writing helpful health and fitness articles, but they complained about how long it took to download it. When it came to inserting images, my philosophy was 'the more the better' and email servers weren't thanking me for it :)

Going live online in 2007!

It was time for a better solution, and clearly this internet thing was where it was at. I purchased a 'website in a box' and went about building my first website under my proudly displayed new business name 'KickAssLife Training'. I wanted the name to encapsulate living your best life and not being just about getting in shape. I was really happy with what I'd come up with.

Building a website was fun! And really quite simple. I felt like I was seriously moving into the big-time and, if I do say so myself, I was pretty impressed with what accomplished, which was a black background with a dizzying array of highlighter-pen type colours and white writing. Ouch :)

I started posting articles, but the site was clunky and difficult to use, so when someone told me I could set up something called a 'blog' for free and that new articles would be updated instantly that seemed the way to go.

I came up with the new business name Play Life Health & Performance Coaching, and the tagline *'Life is Now. Press Play'* (which I still proudly use today!), had a logo designed and I was good to go.

My new site went living around mid-2007 and it didn't take long for me to become seriously addicted to blogging.

It's funny reading through my old posts as I feel like I've pretty much just been repeating myself ever since. I guess I haven't really changed my message :)

Initially I had no concept of making money online. The way I understood it, the main benefit of having an online presence was to build my offline business and more firmly establish me as an expert for when I propositioned businesses to become their in-house training and health guru. I'd also put together some higher-end packages for 'Flying First Class' personal training programs, which involved additional services and support from me outside of training, such as nutrition and life coaching, and I'd written an eBook called 'Stress Less'. I wrote it because my coach said I should write an eBook and set it as a homework assignment, but once written I had no idea what to do with it and so it kind of just sat there gathering dust. Eventually I used it as a free 'opt in' gift on my website.

The Entrepreneurs Weakness: Bright Shiny Ideas

Something you might have noticed about me is that I can't seem to sit still and stick with one idea. This is not exactly a new trait :)

Once I mastered the hang of regular article writing and blog posting, I started to become a little bored with my fairly basic free site. I'd been reading about successful bloggers online and I was stalking their websites. I started to get it into my head that I needed to create something a little more spectacular if I really wanted to make a name for myself and get my writing out there in a bigger way.

The only problem was I just couldn't come up with a business name! For literally 6 months I remained inactive as I journaled and brainstormed almost daily with possible name ideas. I wanted something that I felt would be amazing, that I'd feel incredibly proud of every time I saw it or referred to it, and something that would, of course, sum up what my work could do for people. I honestly think I spent more time coming up with the name for my first 'real' website/blog than what I spent battling to decide on a name for my first child!

But eventually I had it, and it was perfect. 'Body Incredible' was born, and I was so excited. Deciding on the name was just the first part – launching this site was a really big deal to me, it was my 'coming out' as a real writer or at least as someone who fully intended to become a real writer and become known for it. This had been a dream of mine since my childhood years and so I did everything I could to make sure my launch into the online world was perfect.

For another 6 months I worked on collating and editing past articles, and writing new ones. I wanted the site to go live with at least 40 blog posts on it. Articles aside, it had to have the perfect logo and banner, all the right and essential pages, and everything had to work just as it should.

My entire focus was still around my writing, and sharing my message. At no point in my nearly 12-month preparation for Body Incredible did I think about how to make money from it. It was definitely there in the back of my mind, but more as a vague and 'someday' thing, something that seemed very tricky and mysterious and I was quite sure was best held off for the future, when I knew what I was doing.

This was one of just several significant early-on 'would cost me thousands' mistakes in my online business. But more on that later.

It was mid 2008 by this point, and my partner Enzo had opened a brand new restaurant in February of that year. It was a small and beautifully laid out traditional Italian restaurant with food that was to die for, and after its first few weeks had established a name for itself as the place to eat in Melbourne's Eastern Suburbs. It wasn't unusual to have queues for a table going out the door, like a nightclub, and even on a Monday or Tuesday night!

This restaurant was really where Body Incredible was born. During the days I'd train personal training clients from 6am through to 7 or 8pm, stopping on and off for a workout or a snatched half hour on my computer, but it wasn't until 8:30 or 9pm when I reached the restaurant that the magic really began. Night after night and month after month I sat at the bar or at the high stools in the window, a glass of Organic Shiraz on one side and a bowl of warmed olives and almonds on the other (not so great for my computer keyboard!) and I wrote and wrote and wrote.

Regular customers would ask why 'that girl was always alone in the window on her computer'. The restaurant would empty, fill again, empty and fill once more, a distant hum of noise just behind me but feeling as though it was miles away as I lost myself in my work. My wood fired roasted duck with Amarena Cherries and spinach would arrive and without really noticing what I was doing I'd eat it. When I wrote, my entire focus and being was consumed by what I was doing. Hours would pass, the restaurant would empty for the last time the staff would clean up and suddenly Enzo was there saying it was closing time, often past midnight. I'd have had no sense of the time that passed. It was during this time that I really knew – if I didn't already – that writing was what I was born to do.

One night in August 2008 I sat at the bar, talking with a couple of Enzo's friends who were eating there that night, and my focus was not quite as strong as usual. It was ready. There was nothing left to do, I'd triple checked everything, and it was time to open the doors to Body Incredible. I remember being equally elated and also a little letdown that my all-consuming project was now complete.

I was committed to growing this blog and to eventually making something of it from a business perspective. I stuck to a strict blogging schedule, making sure I pre-wrote posts when we were going to be away, and diligently answered every comment and email. The first few times I received an email from someone I didn't know, often sharing their story and thanking me for how I'd helped them, I felt invincible. It was so exciting to be making a mark beyond my own little world!

But despite all of my efforts and diligent work, my little blog grew from having around 80 subscribers after launch (which was my Melbourne network of clients and friends; pre Facebook days!) to having a not-so impressive 109 subscribers by July the year after.

I'd been blogging for a year, was 5 months pregnant with our first child, still working in personal training full time, and getting frustrated. When was it going to be my time?!

I'd even released my first eBook during this time, Secrets of Lasting Weight Loss Revealed – a missive which totals 246 A4 pages and took me over 2 years to complete. I made over $400 the day it launched – 11 sales at US$37 each, and I was blown away thrilled. I thought it was the start of huge things for me – and I guess looking back now it was :) – but the ball that I thought would start rapidly rolling after the release of the eBook stayed stubbornly stuck after that first effort. I felt like I'd done everything and followed all the rules. I'd voraciously read websites like Problogger and Copyblogger from top to toe, enrolled in a Blogging

Mastermind, and implemented everything I learned, like the perfect student I'd always been, and yet I just couldn't break through.

As much as I still loved my writing I was becoming fed up with feeling like I was surgically attached to my laptop, with being the trainer who spent every 5 minutes between clients writing and studying and trying to get ahead while the other trainers kicked back, went for coffees, mucked around in the staff room or had interesting jaunts around the city.

Was it ever going to be worth it? What did I really think I was trying to do anyway? Maybe I just didn't have what it takes.

The Breakthrough

It was around this time that I was extremely lucky to win an online competition whose prize was a half hour 'my blog is broken' consult with one of the biggest names in online marketing at the time, Jon Morrow.

The advice he gave me would quite literally set me on a path that would change my life, and lead me to where I am today, although at the time I had no idea of the power of what he was saying to me and how it could set me on track to making not only hundreds of dollars online each month, but thousands and then eventually tens of thousands.

In just 30 minutes and with just a few simple lines of notes taken I had a plan for my success that was – although I didn't yet know it – going to result in me ending up where I now am today, making over 50k per month consistently online by doing what I love.

Life is Now. Press Play.

How I quit 1:1 PT and created a monthly $50K+ online income - Part 2 – Finally getting traction!

In Part 1 of this series I took you through the first year or two of my online journey – in which I basically blogged my butt off and achieved very little in return, except for a massive audience of 109 subscribers.

I'd reached a point where I was truly starting to wonder if I had what it took, but just when perhaps I may have given up I was fortunate enough to win a competition to have a free consult with one of the internet's most respected writers and editors (amongst other notes of acclaim!), Mr Jon Morrow.

This half hour call literally changed the direction of my online business and I'd go so far as to say changed my life, setting me on a road to creating an online monthly income at times exceeding what I once dreamed of 'hopefully' making in a year from my writing!

Without the meeting with Jon, perhaps I would have continued to battle through and eventually still reached the success I enjoy today – I'd certainly like to think so. But at the same time, I was growing really freaking tired of putting in 20, 30, often 40 hours a week and getting nothing more than 'great feedback' from my personal training clients and the occasional stranger in return.

I wanted more than just great feedback! I wanted it all. And I wanted it now.

And whilst I knew it was possible to create a 'cafe lifestyle' as a successful online entrepreneur, I just had no idea how to make it happen for ME. I felt sure there was something critical I was missing, and it turned out I was right. Although it was not, in retrospect, at all related to the direct advice Jon gave me ...

The Missing Link to My Success

I'll cut to the chase – by implementing Jon's advice I was able to increase my blog traffic by a massive 743% in a matter of weeks. It was the start of something BIG. Jon's advice, as it turned out, was critical when it came to giving me the energy and determination I needed. It was the reaffirmation of the belief that I could do this; I could MAKE it online and that I had a message worth hearing.

Okay, okay, I know you're wanting to know just what it was Jon told me! I have to warn you – it's nothing you haven't heard before. It's just that I took both his advice, and his predicted outcome of following it, absolutely to heart and fully believed in my ability to achieve results.

The consult with Jon took place on February 11th, 2010 – I know that because I still have my file of notes from that day saved on my computer under 'Jon Morrow Advice'. I also have saved a copy of the first guest post I wrote about 6 months afterwards. I thought I'd share it with you here as I outline Jon's advice and also recall the impact it had on my business growth. Here's the post:

In the past 6 months I've created an additional $25,000 in income from blogging, and I'm well on the way to exceeding that figure over the next 6 months. Starting a blog has been one of the most lucrative endeavours I've ever embarked upon.

If you're thinking I seem a little smug about my success, well – you'd be perfectly right :). But before you write me off as one of the lucky ones to whom overnight success just 'happens', let me take you back …

If there's one thing I've learned over the past 3 years it's that blogging success depends on staying power. When I started my first 'real' blog in August 2008, I made one very deliberate commitment to myself. I promised myself I would never, never, never quit. After all, my dream was to be a writer and to make an income from doing so, and blogging seemed a smart path to take. Perhaps, I thought, I might even grow my fitness business along the way.

The first few months saw me wading through various blogging mentoring courses which, while full of great advice, frankly just overwhelmed and even depressed me.

Keeping up with the weekly tasks would have equated to 40+ hours, and I was already working full time for myself as a personal trainer. On top of that, I liked to keep busy with a little exercise, plenty of socialising, and – of course – the requisite 'me-time'. Occasionally I even liked to get a good night's sleep!

If burning myself out doing tasks I didn't really want to do was what it was going to take, then I wasn't really interested. I decided to do things my way, posting consistently 2-3 times per week but otherwise throwing 'the rules' out the window.

Looking back, it wasn't my best choice...

After blogging this way for 10 months, I had an impressive 109 readers. I knew that the definition of madness was to keep doing the same thing repeatedly and expect a different outcome, but I really just didn't know where to start. It was all so overwhelming (and still can be!) I thought that perhaps I should just admit defeat and move on.

Everyone deserves a break now and then.

I'd been thinking that way for a while when I came across a Copyblogger post called 'Screwed up your Blog? Here's what to do.' It was written by Jon Morrow, a blogger and Associate Editor of Copyblogger. The final paragraph had me nearly jumping off my chair:

"Over the next few weeks, I'm going to do around 20-30 telephone consultations. I'll get on the phone with you for

30 minutes, and you can tell me what's troubling you about blogging. I'll then give you advice specific to your exact situation."

What an awesome opportunity! I scrolled past 164 comments and made my entry:

I know you can imagine how over the moon I was when I received an email from Jon saying I'd been chosen. I felt like I'd won the lottery, and literally counted the days until my consult! Looking back, I am convinced that this was the turning point for me. That 30-minute consult is the reason that today, when I release a full-day event at between $200 and $500 a ticket I sell out in weeks. It's the reason I've been able to sell 161 copies of my US$37 e-book, and fill a 12-week telecoaching program in days. Indirectly it's even how I've ended up writing for national publications like The Australian Women's Weekly! And it's allowed me to forge some pretty amazing connections with other bloggers and writers. I still have Jon's advice saved on my computer. In a nutshell, this is what he told me:

Writing guest posts is the best way to build a relationship with another blogger and broaden your audience.

Comments can work as well; best to include a personal life experience

I should come up with a list of 10 blogs relevant to mine, and seek to link my subject matter to theirs when guest posting

Stop writing 3 posts a week for my own blog, and instead write 2 plus 1 guest post

Jon also taught me how to properly pitch a guest post, and gave my confidence a boost by telling me my writing was good enough to pitch to blogs with 30,000+ subscribers!

Back to the Grind

So it was back to the grind for me, but with a real vengeance! I could do this. I would do this! And the best part was, I could do it by employing my existing skills, not by figuring out every in and out of online marketing or blog design!

As you can see, the key piece of advice Jon gave me was to broaden my reach by guest posting weekly and leaving regular comments. I certainly implemented Jon's advice to the letter, and when I tallied the outcomes in the above article half a year later I was convinced that my traffic growth and resulting financial success was due entirely to these two weekly or daily actions.

It wasn't until years later that I realised it was the less strategy-based side of my conversation and follow-up emails and Skype communications with Jon that was the real key to my success. In fact, the true gift that he gave me was something I now consider to be one of the top 2 overall reasons I've reached the heights I have after now 7 years online ...

In the meantime, I did attribute my somewhat rapid growth to the relentless pitching of my work. Through 2010 I wrote many guest posts, some of them for major blogs like Dumb Little Man and Pick the Brain, some for smaller and lesser known sites. I pitched everyone, and sometimes I wasn't answered, but most of the time the response was encouraging.

A key lesson from this period was how important it is to persist even when you're not getting the results you want. Sometimes I'd find myself knocked back weeks in a row – it would have been easy to give up but I kept my eyes firmly focused on just continuing to put one foot in front of the other. I had my confidence back and was newly convinced that if I simply refused to give up I would succeed.

Really, and I'm sure I don't have to tell you – what Jon had taught me wasn't rocket science. I just hadn't heard this stuff specific to me. I hadn't been told 'you can do this; you've got what it takes', and I think that's what made the difference for me.

I felt empowered and it gave me the energy I needed to keep going. Jon's advice – and the results I got when I truly took it to heart – gave me the motivation I needed to spend 2010 building a blog with close to 2000 subscribers and getting my name out there as someone to reckon with.

I remember proudly the day one of the 'net's biggest regular bloggers' at the time Ali Hale commented to me that "you're everywhere at the moment". "Yes I am!" I thought.

"And this is just the beginning"

But Where Was The BIG Money?!

Despite how rapidly I was able to grow my readership after following Jon's advice I still didn't really make any 'real' money in 2010.

That being said, I did okay. I was a baby in the world of online and – unlike most start-ups today – I had no online community, mastermind, regular coach or forum. I wasn't even on Facebook yet! I was figuring things out alone and most of the ideas I had I dreamed up myself. Looking back I am in some ways grateful for the chance to truly pave my own way – these days it seems we are inundated all day, every day with all the things we could or should be doing online to get ahead, and it can be exhausting to say the least.

At the time it did feel as though I was doing it the tough way in some regards. I was rapt to have my name out there, have my subscribers list build daily and to have some modest financial success, but I still felt that I'd only just tapped my potential. I was committed to being seriously successful as an entrepreneur and I wasn't going to stop until I got there!

By this time it was 2011 and I was still working pretty much full-time as a busy personal trainer as well as having several apprentices working for me as well.

While this was a great boost financially it was also a relentless demand of my attention, and not really what I wanted to be doing with my time. What I wanted to be doing, was hiding away by myself and making money from my writing! And I have to say my primary 'want' hasn't really changed since then at all :)

At times it seemed that maybe I just wasn't going to have that breakthrough that I was longing for. Was it ever going to be MY time in a seriously BIG way?

I won't say I was really ready to give up or even that I was properly disheartened; I think it was more of a case of having become 'used' to spending a lot of my spare time planning and working on my blog, and because I didn't have personal connection with anyone who was truly making it or doing anything except blogging and working on an eBook, it never entered my head that things could be a LOT easier than this and that I could make not just a living but create serious abundance and financial freedom through my blog.

A Big (and Thrilling!) Breakthrough

One day I was checking my emails and I saw the name 'Sarah Wilson' in my inbox. Sarah Wilson was – and is – a journalist and blogging 'celebrity' in Australia, and she was someone I'd long admired for her writing career. I would even say she was kind of an idol to me. At first I thought the name was just a coincidence, so you can imagine how excited I was when I opened it to see that it was, in fact, from 'the' Sarah Wilson! She'd come across my writing on one of the US blogs I'd been frequently guest posting on, and she got in touch pretty much just to say 'hi' and (OMG!!) "You're a great writer, do you currently write for any magazines?"

I was blown away and honestly I felt like a little kid at Christmas. My idol was coming to ME telling me I was good and saying I should be writing for magazines! What were the odds of that?!

Over the next few months we bounced emails back and forth – at the time Sarah was just starting to build her blog and we even spoke about that. In the meantime, Sarah recommended me to ACP; one of Australia's largest publishing houses and I ended up with a paid gig with the Australian Women's Weekly which lasted 2 years. Not exactly my core market, but still – how cool! And so exciting to be paid for my articles.

I'd also won a few competitions over at the Dumb Little Man blog, where they gave monetary rewards for the guest posts which got the most hits each month.

I was starting to feel like maybe I could really make it as a writer, but I was still thinking small; along the lines of being paid $100 or $200 here or there for an article. Not for a moment had I even begun to fathom just how far my little blog would one day take me.

I was just thrilled to be seeing results in terms of my subscriber list, and to know I was starting to 'make it' as a writer.

By this time I'd given birth to our first child – in late 2009 – and life had become even crazier. My 'Secrets of Lasting Weight Loss Revealed' book continued to sell a few copies, but my overall income was looooowww as I was not seeing clients after giving birth, and even when I started to do so it was only a session or two here or there. I still had 2 apprentices working for me as trainers and was grateful for the money I made from that but really tired of having to be there for people when I had a brand new baby to look after.

My First Online 'e' Program

I decided it was time to take things to another level, and so in July of 2010 I launched my first online program – Body Incredible Health Telecoaching. Yes, a very glamorous name!

I'd never come across the notion of writing a sales page or truly marketing to a defined niche :) But again, I didn't know what I didn't know and I was thrilled with the results.

I made around 6 or 7 grand from this 12-week program and I honestly just thought it was too good to be true that I could generate over $500 an hour for a group phone coaching call coupled with putting together a weekly worksheet.

In the middle of the program we took off for a 6-week and amazing trip around the US and Canada, during which we also eloped in 'The Valley of Fire' just outside Las Vegas.

It was amazing – we'd long planned the Vegas thing and basically we spent the money we would have used for a wedding on traveling instead. I still remember being in Canada at Enzo's relatives home and doing my telecoaching call back to my students in Australia – it was my first experience of 'making money no matter where you are in the world' and it was a big thrill as well as an insight into just what was possible in this online world.

Back to Full-Time Personal Training ... and About to Turn a Corner in a BIG Way!

We returned from our overseas trip in late October of 2010, and I pretty much threw myself back into full-time personal training.

After all, that was how I *knew* how to make money fast, so I figured it was what had to be done. It didn't take more than a few weeks before the relaxation of our long getaway wore off and I realised with a moment of finality that 13 or so years of personal training was really enough. I didn't want to be doing this anymore. When I was with my clients I had a great time, but the truth is that when I wasn't with them – and was writing – was when I was truly living. I'd feel myself float away into another world with my writing and when other trainers came to let me know my next client was there, or when I was working in a cafe early in the morning before my first 7am client I noticed the time, I'd feel resentful and grumpy at being interrupted.

It was time to get more serious. It was time to start pushing myself to take risks and – like a mother bird pushing her baby out of the nest – to push myself over that ledge and away from all that I knew and all that felt safe and comfortable and most of all achievable.

And whilst I had no clue at the time, I was about to turn a corner in a big way. In fact, I was about to do something pretty damn crazy that would look like pure madness, but ultimately be pivotal in my online income going from a few hundred per month to a few thousand per month over the next 12 months, and then a few tens of thousands per month over the following year!

In the next post:

How I came up with the idea for my first truly successful online business 'Woman Incredible', how I launched that business so as to achieve close to 1000 subscribers on my first day, and how I created over $30,000 of online income in the year to come.

The true gift that Jon Morrow gave me and how THAT was really what set me on the path to success rather than simply guest posting and commenting. (You may have already guessed what this was).

My crazy spur of the moment decision that looked like absolute madness at the time and ultimately allowed me to increase my income tenfold in the 12 months to follow

Life is Now. Press Play.

Have you ever had one of those ideas that you just know is going to change your life?

That's exactly how I felt back in 2011 when – after nearly 4 years battling it out online and for the most part not really getting anywhere – I hit upon the idea of Woman Incredible. At the time I was just so darn excited to have something to be excited about again! It felt great to wake up naturally early each morning, already pumped to get to work building my new blog and community, and to go to bed each night with my mind full of ideas for the next day.

Little did I know that my 'cool idea' would soon turn into over $30,000 of quickly created income and then into a quarter of a million dollar business!

In today's blog – Part 3 of my Business Story series – I want to share the story of Woman Incredible with you and how I was able to go from making a 'modest' online income to making a truly abundant and lifestyle changing living that allowed me to finally quit my 1:1 business in just over a year.

The True Lesson Jon Morrow Taught Me

In the last post I shared the exact advice that online writer and editor extraordinaire Jon Morrow gave me in the half hour consult I won with him. It was great advice and I could literally credit an over 700% increase in my blog traffic over the 6 months following that consult to his advice. I also made what I considered my first real money online in that year – over $10,000 between a telecoaching program and my eBook 'Secrets of Lasting Weight Loss Revealed'.

I was pumped! Of course :) But it wasn't until years later – perhaps not even until I sat down to write this series – that I realised what the true gift was that Jon gave me.

He gave me back the ability to believe in myself.

I'd become so used to doing the hard yards online, to blogging and blogging and dutifully trying to implement the Never-Ending List of Things That Must Be Done to Make It Online (I know you've seen that list!) that I guess I was just used to the battle. But as much as I didn't mind working hard and I certainly did love writing and engaging with my community, I was getting tired.

Our daughter had come along to add a ton of joy to our lives but also (as kids often do) a big wake up call. I didn't want to be doing Personal Training for the rest of my life, trading time for money – not even for a great hourly wage. And to be perfectly honest, I didn't even want to be doing it for another month, week or even day!

I wanted an out. Not because I didn't enjoy life as it was then but because I believed it could be so much more of what I really craved. Which was freedom. Choice. The ability to live life 100% on my terms. And to 'make it' as a writer, to achieve success and recognition by empowering others to recognise what THEY really wanted out of life and then to give them the drive to go out and achieve it.

But how could I even contemplate teaching something like that when I wasn't making MY dream business and life a reality?!

I had become used to feeling stuck, overloaded, as though sheer hard slog and VERY slow growth was the only way to get ahead.

After my conversation with Jon – especially as he complimented me repeatedly on the quality of my writing – I felt like I could take on the world! Do anything! Isn't it amazing how much an attitude and self-belief change can impact on the actual results you create?

I guess it's not so amazing really, not with what I now know about dream life creation and getting what you expect. But at the time it was just such a relief to be told 'you can do this'.

'You've got what it takes'.

I really needed to hear it. And I want to tell you right now, particularly if you're reading this feeling inspired and hopeful but also a little scared that maybe you don't have what it takes.

You can do this.

You have what it takes.

And it is absolutely WORTH this battle that you're going through now.

But let's talk about how to fast-track success.

Despite being able to create over 10k income from my site Body Incredible (which was all about nutrition, exercise and motivation) I was missing one key thing.

When I work with my business mentoring clients now, one of the very first things we do is get absolutely clear on niche and ideal client. Let me be upfront – most people have done this exercise. Yet despite this, most people are absolutely NOT clear on niche and ideal client, are holding stuff back and also not really letting THEIR true identity shine through in their online business.

One of the easiest ways to fail fast online is to try to be like everyone else, or even anyone else and that's what I was learning. I wasn't particularly modelling myself after anybody online (at the time I didn't really know of any other trainers with blogs!) but I was basically churning out fairly standard content based on what I would learn in various courses, with the occasional 'real Kat' mindset or personal development piece thrown in.

My light wasn't really shining very brightly at all, and to make things worse I was trying to appeal to anyone who wanted to lose weight. Yep ... kind of a big market :)

For several years I'd been resisting this little voice inside of me telling me that I needed to specialise in working with women. I didn't want to be that girl! I actually preferred my male personal training clients to my female – less chit-chat :)

But at the same time I was starting to realise I had an important message to share with women. And that it ran so much deeper than simply 'fat loss and nutrition' stuff. Despite becoming attuned to this fact I stubbornly resisted the idea for a good 6 months, maybe more. And looking back, I'm not even sure what changed. I just know that at some point I knew I had to move on from Body Incredible and create a community for women.

For months – seriously, nearly 6 months – I brainstormed to try and come up with a name for my female-only venture. I was very close to buying moneysexchocolate.com ... I got it into my head that those were all the things women wanted more of and so that it was therefore an infallible business idea!

Fortunately (I guess?!) I moved on from that idea and kept beating my head against the wall for a few months before it hit me. So simple. So obvious. So perfect. My site Body Incredible had taken me on a great ride, and I still loved the name. I was a little sad to be leaving it behind. And so came the birth of Woman Incredible –

This time around there was no WAY I was going in unprepared. I knew so much more about making it online than back in '07 when my first little newsletter-turned-blog went online and this time I was in it for more than just an outlet for my writing and a way to give a broader service to my clients.

Those long-awaited dreams of being a truly FREE

entrepreneur were about to come to fruition. I could just FEEL it. Oh sure, I'd been working for myself the whole time anyhow but anyone who has done 1:1 as a business model knows it's really just a well-paid job. As soon as you stop, so does the money. And 'freedom' or 'choice' are not exactly words we associate with a busy 1:1 practice. At least I didn't!

I saw Woman Incredible as my way out of the successful-but-way-too-full-on-and-unsustainable life I'd created for myself. My daughter was a year old, I'd come back from our 6-week US and Canada elopement trip feeling refreshed only to right away realise I didn't WANNA be doing PT anymore, and I was filled with motivation and perhaps an over-inflated idea of what I could achieve online after the 25k or so success I'd had in 2010.

It was time. It was MY time. Not only to finally create the freedom and choice I longed for but to truly start writing the stuff I wanted to write and make a difference. And somehow I just knew that this was going to be big.

I spent close to 6 months preparing to launch Woman Incredible. Everything had to be just right.

I had a logo designed which I still LOVE – despite us speaking 2 different languages, the guy I hired got the exact effect I was going for (after about 30 edits, no wonder he didn't want to work with me again afterwards haha - as someone who never stops changing her mind I'm a graphic designers nightmare; he wouldn't be the only one to say it lol)

I pre-wrote 16 blog posts (the plan being to publish 2 a week), based around the idea that I wanted to take my readers through an internal shift over the first 6 months of the blog, so I'd written out themes on what I would cover each month.

I carefully put together a series of pages covering my philosophies on all of the different areas Woman Incredible would be about – nutrition, stress, motivation and mindset, exercise, and of course the big one – 'you'.

And this time around I even wrote a tentative plan for how I was going to turn this thing into a business.

After how long it took me to get traffic traction on Body Incredible I decided to be really strategic about launching Woman Incredible, and so I invited basically every fabulous nutrition/mindset/fitness based woman I knew or knew of online to join the launch, and also put together a giveaway package worth over $900 for each of my first 100 subscribers.

On top of that I'd been talking about the launch and what I was up to on Body Incredible for ages. Even though I'd never really heard of or studied launch processes and certainly didn't know what a 'pre-launch' was, that's basically what I was doing.

And it worked! On March 1, 2011 at 11am Melbourne time Woman Incredible and the accompanying Facebook page went live. Well – it nearly did :) If you've ever planned a launch done to the minute you'll know something ALWAYS goes wrong! At the designated time I was having coffee with a client who was visiting from Perth (and had brought me amazing flowers to celebrate Woman Incredible) and ... nothing happened on Woman Incredible but my 'it's here!' email still went out to Body Incredible fans. Not the last time I've fumbled a launch!

Anyway, that was soon fixed and by the end of that day I believe I had close to 1000 email subscribers and several hundred Facebook fans – 283 I believe was the number!

Fast forward to now – 2.5 years later – and that's turned into over 13k email subscribers, over 22k Facebook fans, over 50k per month of consistent online income, and a community of incredible women all working together to change their bodies and change their LIVES.

Yes. I'm a little bit proud :)

But the thing I was MOST proud and excited about was that finally I felt I'd found my flow.

Recently I read that the definition of happiness is waking up feeling optimistic and expectant about the day you get to live and that's exactly how I felt throughout my entire build up to launching Woman Incredible, as well as in the early days after it came to life. I just couldn't get enough of writing. Day after day I'd be lost in what I was doing, glued to my laptop screen as I sat in funky inner Melbourne cafes, or occasionally at home, and just wrote and wrote and wrote.

When I was in that world, honestly the building next to me could have fallen down and I wouldn't have noticed. Hours could pass and suddenly I'd realise my coffee was long cold, I'd been busting to go to the bathroom for over an hour, and the cafe staff were starting to give me 'that' look.

I'd found my bliss and if I didn't know it before I certainly knew then that I was BORN to be a writer.

It's funny how when you find something you're so passionate about – so meant to do – that you become incredibly motivated with all areas of your life, you become more motivated outside of just that thing. Even before the 'birth day' of Woman Incredible I felt incredibly empowered and inspired with what was possible for this business – and filled with ideas! One of those ideas – something I was SURE would make me my fortune online and at the same really help me to share my message and make a difference was to create a membership program for women who really wanted to take charge of their fitness and health and work with me more closely.

I spent 6 months working on the creation of my Woman Incredible VIP Platinum Mentoring program and finally launched it at 6pm on my birthday, October 2 – 6 days and 1 month after the launch of the site.

It was pretty stressful launching it at a specific time! My business manager Mal (who had started part time with me in July that year) and I literally pressed publish on the final piece of the puzzle at 5.59pm – the 'it's here' email was going live right on 6pm and I had to be at my birthday dinner at 6.30! You'd think I would have learned about launching things at specific times by now but I still keep doing it to this day ... and it NEVER gets any less stressful :) the only difference now is that I've learned (and Mal has also!) that this is just how I get things done – always down to the wire.

My $75K Program Launch!

I guess I'd done something right with my pre-launch 'building anticipation' as in the 3 days that I kept the doors of VIP open I had over 100 people register! The 'deal' was $1 only for the first month and then $97 per month after that, for a total of 12 months. Yep – my very first real program was a 12 month program in which members received the following every single day:

- Motivational email
- Nutrition/transformation tip for the day
- Motivation action task/journaling for the day
- Daily workout video for home or gym (yep every single day!)
- Weekly recipes
- Weekly meal plans

- Plus my VIP ladies had access to a TON of additional resources and bonuses, with new ones coming out monthly. I don't do things by halves! The program is one I still run once a year and it comprises 18 2-5 week learning modules over the year – the idea is not just that you receive daily workout and food 'how-to' and 'what to' but also that you go through a process of learning and understanding what YOU need to know on everything from finding your unique food needs, to hormones, to stress, digestion and a ton of other aspects of health. Basically I tried to compress everything I know about health and being in shape into this program.

After the $1 trial month I had just over 40 ladies stay on – a result I was pretty happy about, although by month 4-5 a few more had dropped off.

At the time I thought this was terrible and I couldn't understand why – the program was SO comprehensive. In retrospect I now know that it was way TOO comprehensive for most people. Can you imagine receiving a daily (long!) email of tasks and learning for your business? Every day?! It sounds good in theory but would you actually read and implement every day; I know I wouldn't! In the end I cut the emails down to 5 per week but it is definitely still a program for those who want results and to also LEARN and create a lifestyle approach to their health and nutrition, not just for those who want quick-fix results.

I've also learned that it's basically the norm for people to start dropping off in month 4 when it comes to programs 6 months or longer. So I feel better about that!

I went live with the program again 6 months after its first launch, using the same $1 deal, and the income result from these combined open periods was over $70,000! You can imagine how stoked I was, especially after how much WORK its creation was.

It literally took an entire year to finish putting together, as I basically created the content day by day as we went, and filmed videos in batches every 3 weeks. I came to absolutely DREAD those filming days – it took all day and I found it tedious. It was a real lesson that my preferred way to work is to be completely unbound by appointments and 'have to do today's!' Plus – I really just want to write and not do anything else!

As for the daily emails with all their content and the recipes, meal plans, module overviews and reports etc. – I did that entirely on the fly. I mean it – when the program went live I'd written 'Daily Digest #1' and that was IT. After that I tried to get a few days or sometimes a week ahead but often I was writing the days digest on the same day it had to go out. This went on for the entire 12 months – we might have at one stage been 2 weeks ahead when I was going away, but that was it!

I was really hard on myself about being so 'disorganised' and doing everything at the last minute.

I'd initially planned to write the whole year in advance

(GOD!) but it just seemed that old high-school version of me who did all her big assignments the night before was stronger than the 'wants to be organised and pre-prepared' side of me!

The funny thing is – now that I hang out with so many incredibly successful female entrepreneurs in online masterminds I know it's really, really common for people to create their programs on the fly. You might think the idea sounds horrific (and scary!) but there's a certain type of creative who just loves that type of 'under pressure' approach to work.

It's been just over 2 years now since I launched VIP and in that time I've gone live with 3 other major eCourse programs and with each and every one I've created as I go. I've come to terms with that being my creation style – and so has Mal. She hasn't had any other choice haha :)

Already looking for the next challenge ...

As awesome as VIP was and as great as the testimonials and feedback from it were in those early months it was quickly apparent that it wasn't going to be the 'thing that everybody would do' that I'd hoped for. It was obvious that most people wanted something far less complex and more specific to their current need. I was starting to get more and more requests on both Facebook and email to write up a 'list of allowed foods', so in January of 2012 I started doing just that.

Being the details kind of gal that I am, my list of foods

quickly became a full-blown report which then turned into an eating plan with every possible accompaniment you can imagine, from shopping lists, to detailed meal plans and recipes, to food prep tips, to rules on 'treat meals', to calculating how much protein you need and even to understanding your motivation and any sabotage issues when it comes to eating right and so The Look Great Naked Eating Plan was born.

Around the same time that I was writing my eating plan I made an incredible, spontaneous and what felt like crazy decision to walk out of doing personal training. I was having a massage after a massive day of clients, and my mind was running crazy as I tried to 'jigsaw' all the components of my busy life into a plan that seemed workable.

I was tired of the relentless 1:1 days, and had been for some time. Not only did I want more freedom, I wanted to be able to spread a bigger message and now that I was starting to do that with Woman Incredible I resented being restrained by having so much of my limited 'work' time (my daughter was only a little over a year old so I couldn't work 24/7 like I used to!) taken up by stuff that held no deeper purpose.

At the same time I had this constant sense that if only I could bring myself to the plunge and make a leap of faith that I'd be able to create something truly remarkable and entirely on my terms. I spent nearly the entire massage hour trying to work out how to fit in everything I wanted to do, and even make space for new projects, and suddenly it hit me:

It wasn't going to happen.

And it was up to me to do something NOW to create the life I claimed I wanted. I walked out of that massage room certain that I had to quit PT, and on Monday, three days afterwards I did just that. Two weeks later and I was done – over 13 years of personal training finished, just like that. It was an incredibly bittersweet time, and also an incredibly exhilarating feeling to know that I was literally putting my life in my own hands.

I'd decided to jump with no idea what was ahead and by God I was going to make sure it worked out.

Little did I know that big success was already just around the corner for me. Little did I know that those offhand requests for a 'list of allowed foods' which led to me creating my Eating Plan would be the start of my building an online empire via The Look Great Naked Training Plan, The Look Great Naked Bootcamp and a myriad of other related products and offerings.

In fact, by the time 2012 drew to an end that leap of faith would have paid off in a way I'd never dreamed possible and I'd be making upwards of $30,000 per MONTH.

Life is Now. Press Play.

Before You Leave This Chapter!

One sentence: write down what you are thinking right now about your business dreams. Write it from the point of view of what you are most inspired to create. This is simple foundation work to start getting all those ideas and lurking thoughts out of your head, and is important to do regardless of whether you're completely new to online business or you've been going for years. If you want to take things to the next level in business or in life, get in the habit of asking yourself what you want, honestly and often.

CHAPTER THREE – FOR GUARANTEED RESULTS, START HERE

The mindset work you do each day - and it really should be EACH day; just as showering and eating should be each day! - is what will guarantee your success far and beyond the We're about to dive into some pretty serious strategy and tactics.

What I'm going to teach you, if you apply it consistently, has the power to create everything you can imagine for your business not only financially but also in terms of 'soul satisfaction' and truly living the dream in your life and lifestyle.

But first, we need to make sure you have the most powerful strategy of all, and that your most transformative tool is tuned and ready. I'm talking, of course, about your mind.

Think about what an athlete might do before they go onto the field to compete. They might spend some time warming up physically, but what else do they do? They get themselves ready for battle. They psych themselves into an attitude of success. They rev themselves up so that when they DO charge onto the field it's with a battle cry and a certain determination that they WILL prevail.

You don't necessarily have to turn on your laptop each morning with a battle cry, but to be honest? You gotta come pretty close. Who do you think is more likely to succeed?

The woman who logs on each morning sighing to herself about all that there is to do, and feeling weighed down at the heaviness of it all and depressed about 'not getting results yet'?

Or the woman who, regardless of her current results, takes some time to change her mind and emotions. To build faith, trust, expectation and determination. To remind herself of why she is here, and why she is doing this work.

It's pretty obvious right?

And if you think that hard work alone is the key to success, you're bound for disappointment. If you truly desire to create your dreams then you KNOW that also means dealing with challenges, self-sabotage, blocks and fears along the way and it also means taking action even when you don't know what to do!

The mindset work you do each day – and it really should be

EACH day; just as showering and eating should be each day! – is what will guarantee your success far beyond the actual work you put in.

So tell me -

Are you willing to do what it takes to achieve what YOU desire for your business and life? Are you truly willing to move forward, 'come what may'?

Are you READY?

Are you prepared to get uncomfortable?

Are you prepared to keep taking action even when you're flying blind?

Are you willing to enlist the right support, push past your failures, and just. Keep. Going. Are You?

If you can say yes to ALL of the above, then congratulations. You're in the right place. And this is just the beginning.

Before You Leave This Chapter!

Here is one of my favourite journaling exercises you can turn to when you need to build self-belief, and determination. Think of it as your 'battle cry' exercise!

Find Your Why: take some time to write about your true underlying motivation for creating business success on your terms. Try to get to the real 'core' of your why rather than just the surface reasons such as making money, or creating a great lifestyle. What is it REALLY about? What are the emotions and feelings you long to create through your successful business?

The deeper you can go into exploring your internal reasons for doing what you do, the easier it is to keep moving forward and stay motivated even when the going gets tough.

Hint: for more on this sort of mindset work, make sure you pick up Book 1 in the 'Think Like a Rich Chick' series, which is: Think Like a Rich Chick! And Create Your Millionaire Mindset!

CHAPTER FOUR – WHAT'S YOUR DREAM BIZ? HOW TO FIND IT, AND START IT!

If you're a creative sort of person, as I am, you probably have a mind that at times seems to race at a billion miles an hour, churning out ideas and 'bright shiny objects'.

I remember a couple of years back going on a 5-night getaway with our extended family and not taking my laptop with me. I decided I should 'switch off' for a few days. Since I hate starting the day (especially if it's a day filled with other people!) without first having time for me, I made a point of getting up at 530am each day and walking the 20 minutes into town and the beach. I spent about 20 minutes doing a little workout on the beach and then went and had coffee with nothing but my phone and my thoughts for company. I thought it might be good for me to be forced to just sit and relax and 'be' for once, rather than constantly be DOING or creating.

If you ever find yourself stuck for ideas and creative flow in your business, I can tell you with certainty that the best thing you can do is put yourself in a situation where you have nothing but your own thoughts for an hour or so each day, and some way of taking notes - by the time that 5 day getaway was over I had over 100 notes on my phone for business ideas!

And I was damn EXCITED about them as well. I was doing research throughout the day while sitting round the pool with family and was all prepared to start important hair care products specific to gym junkies. I think I even registered a domain name! And that was just one of the ideas :)

As a matter of fact, I don't think I'd be exaggerating to say I have well over 100 domain names registered. Be honest now - are you smiling because you think I'm a crazy person or because as a fellow creative you can relate?!

Perhaps you don't have 100 business ideas registered but I'll bet you've had over 100 ideas run through your mind over the years. Maybe you are already absolutely clear on your business vision and what you want to do. But maybe you are kind of jumping from thought to thought, not sure where to start or what would be viable. Maybe you're even doing that despite already HAVING a business! Or perhaps you feel like any ideas you have had are just silly, or too wishy-washy, or 'you won't be able to make money doing that'.

Want the good news? By the time you finish this chapter you'll have made a definite decision about your business name, purpose, and clientele. Better still, this will be about launching (or fine-tuning) your DREAM business, where you get to make an awesome living (and then some!) by doing what you love and are most called to do.

That's what it's really about, after all!

So first things first. Know this:

Pretty much any possible business idea you can imagine, is viable. There's a market for just about anything and everything, so you don't really need to ever ask yourself if your idea is a 'good' idea. You only need to ask yourself if it's a good idea FOR YOU.

Here's a quick 'cheat sheet' to starting the right business.

(And don't worry, I'll go into more detail after this, but it's an important start!)

What's the idea; or even the gist of it?

Does it feel right?

Would you quite happily talk about or teach about that topic even if it weren't your business?

Do you find yourself naturally talking about it to

family/friends/anyone who'll listen?

If money were not an issue, and you never had to work again, would you be happy to spend your time on this idea?

In your spare time, do you read about or otherwise invest your energy into topics related to your idea?

Does it feel right?! (Yes, I'm asking that twice - I firmly believe that intuition is the most powerful tool at your disposal, when it comes to creating the right business for you).

Let's get specific now: What's your business about?

Here's the thing. If I give you a week to come up with the perfect business idea, you'll take a week. And if I give you a year, you could very well take a year. As a matter of fact, you may well be where you are right now - i.e. not yet 'living' your dream biz for the very reason that you HAVE been giving yourself all the time in the world to really 'figure it out', even though you might not have been doing so consciously.

If you've been:

- Procrastinating...
- Waiting...
- Resisting...

In any way, shape or form in your business then it simply

has to stop. The very best way to move forward in your business is to move forward! And trust that by doing so you will FIGURE OUT THE RIGHT ANSWERS AS YOU GO.

But you sure as heck won't figure them out by dilly-dallying and not taking any 'real action'! Wouldn't you rather launch a product or program and realise afterwards that it's not quite right - or possibly even completely not right - than NOT launch anything, ever and continue to wait for some sort of divine message about what you should do?!

Okay then.

So. We're going to do this real quick. Kinda like ripping off a band aid, yes? But here's the real kicker: whatever you write down now, you are going to COMMIT to actually following through on. Right away. Meaning that as you work through this book you will actually be CREATING that business, and products for it.

Bit scary? Good! It's all about the action-taking beautiful, and there's no rule that says you can't change things as you go, but if you fail to begin until you're 'sure' you'll never get there. And even if you do at some point decide you're sure? It's a certainty that you'll still end up changing your mind! Remember, making up your mind and taking action doesn't 'lock you in' for life, but it does ensure you move forward and that's really what we want right now!

For each of the below questions, give yourself no more than 60 seconds to come up with some sort of answer. DON'T SECOND GUESS YOURSELF. I'm asking each question as though your business doesn't yet exist - even if it already does, I'd like you to answer the questions this way as we are still talking about some sort of evolution from where you are now to where you truly would LOVE to be.

Start Your Dream Biz Questions:

Pull out paper and pen and hop to it!

What will your business do?

What will you sell? (List as many options as you like)

Suggested name of the business?

Tagline?

What is YOUR 'why' for running this business? I.e. why is it important to you to do so (including financial and 'recognition' reasons as well as intrinsic reasons)

What will you do that is different from what others in your industry do? How will you stand out?

These next questions are about your audience, and who you will serve.

Answer them just as quickly.

Who is your business designed for?

What will they come to you for?

What do they need and also want more than anything right now?

What is their biggest problem right now?

Why should they work with you?

What is the first way you will help them (i.e. an entry level or free product they can download)

Why do you really 'get' and want to help this group of people?

Getting Real for the Long-Term

If you truly want to create your dream business, where you get to enjoy:

- The money
- Any recognition or fame you desire
- And the lifestyle, but also -
- Soul satisfaction
- A sense of being 'on purpose'
- Being able to work from a place of passion and flow
- Feeling aligned, and knowing you are doing what you were meant to do
- Being able to make the rules and do things entirely

on your terms -

Then you need to make sure you go into business, or go into the next stage of your business, with all of these things in mind. Work to maintain a constant vision of the business and life you truly want, and your underlying reasons for doing it. This might take the form of daily journaling to remind you of why you're doing what you're doing, or meditation or daydreaming, or creating a vision board, perhaps, showing everything you're working to create in your life. There are many ways you can connect with the inner you and with your true desires. It doesn't matter which you use, it matters only that you regularly take time to focus your mind, energies and emotions on what you TRULY are working to create. Fail to do this and you risk falling into the pattern that so many entrepreneurs before you have succumbed to, which is to chase endless lists of things that 'should' be done and to end up (often unwittingly, but still) focusing on ways that appear the best for money-making purposes rather than alignment purposes.

As a side note on this, I've found it to be true beyond a shadow of a doubt - and not just in my life but also my clients lives - that when you create a business from a place of alignment and continue growing it by doing what you are MEANT to do rather than what you 'should' do, you will find far greater financial success anyway.

So you may as well save yourself the hassle and start your dream biz in the first place - and then KEEP it your dream biz by constantly tuning in!

If right now some part of you is thinking it would be too good to be true to get to 'do what you love' and make a killing at it, you need to go ahead and squash that belief right now. The world is filled with examples of people who are making a ton of money by doing what they love, so why not choose examples and inspiration by looking to people like that and ignoring any examples of people who have created their so-called wealth by living with year after year of regret, and eventually dying with their light still inside of them.

You get to choose what you believe in this world.

And what you believe ALWAYS comes true.

So right now, make up your mind that you CAN succeed at creating your dream business and not only that but that you WILL. You don't have to know how. You just have to commit to making it happen, and decide in advance that you will persevere until you get there.

If you'd like to know more about how to turn your thoughts in the direction of true success on your terms I highly recommend you download one of my other books in this series, which is 'Think Like a Rich Chick! And Create Your Millionaire Mindset'.

For now, know this -

You are allowed to be successful doing what you love.

You can create business success entirely on your terms.

You can do so in a way that works for you not just 'when you get there', but now. This means that if you crave mornings to yourself, you can have them! If you hate writing but find the idea of making video blogs cool, then you can choose video as your method of communication. If you want 3 days off a week, take it! Whatever you would like from a lifestyle or success point of view is possible, you just need to go out there and make it happen!

Before You Leave This Chapter!

I have one last 'answer very quickly' exercise for you. Grab your journal or notebook, and pen, and tell me (don't think, just write!) - What are the qualities or 'must haves' of your dream business? What I mean is, the things that are essential to you, either intrinsically or extrinsically.

For example - a certain amount of income, stability (define it), feeling 'on purpose', creativity, newness, working at certain times and not others, and so on. Anything and everything that comes to mind as 'THAT would be awesome'. Write down at least 10 things. Do it now!

CHAPTER FIVE – YOU CAN TELL A WINNER BY THE LOOK IN THEIR EYES

This chapter is an extract from my blog. If you ever struggle with determination and motivation to just keep going, you need to read this.

What Do You See When You Look in The Mirror?

You can tell a winner by the look in their eyes.

There's a famous story that perhaps you've heard. Napoleon Hill shares it in his book 'Think and Grow Rich'.

'Shortly after Mr. Darby received his degree from the "University of Hard Knocks" and had decided to profit by his experience in the gold mining business, he had the good fortune to be present on an occasion that proved to him that “No” does not necessarily mean no.

One afternoon he was helping his uncle grind wheat in an old fashioned mill. The uncle operated a large farm on which a number of black sharecrop farmers lived. Quietly, the door was opened, and a small child, the daughter of a tenant, walked in and took her place near the door.

The uncle looked up, saw the child, and barked at her roughly, “What do you want?”

Meekly, the child replied, “My mammy say send her fifty cents.”

“I'll not do it,” the uncle retorted, “Now you run on home.”

“Yas sah,” the child replied. But she did not move. The uncle went ahead with his work, so busily engaged that he did not pay enough attention to the child to observe that she did not leave. When he looked up and saw her still standing there, he yelled at her, “I told you to go on home! Now go, or I'll take a switch to you.”

The little girl said “yas sah,” but she did not budge an inch. The uncle dropped a sack of grain he was about to pour into the mill hopper, picked up a barrel stave, and started toward the child with an expression on his face that indicated trouble.

Darby held his breath. He was certain he was about to witness a murder. He knew his uncle had a fierce temper. He knew that black children were not supposed to defy white people in that part of the country.

When the uncle reached the spot where the child was standing, she quickly stepped forward one step, looked up into his eyes, and screamed at the top of her shrill voice, "MY MAMMY'S GOTTA HAVE THAT FIFTY CENTS!"

The uncle stopped, looked at her for a minute, then slowly laid the barrel stave on the floor, put his hand in his pocket, took out half a dollar, and gave it to her. The child took the money and slowly backed toward the door, never taking her eyes off the man whom she had just conquered.

After she had gone, the uncle sat down on a box and looked out the window into space for more than ten minutes. He was pondering, with awe, over the whipping he had just taken. Mr. Darby, too, was doing some thinking. That was the first time in all his experience that he had seen a black child deliberately master a white adult.

How did she do it? What happened to his uncle that caused him to lose his fierceness and become as docile as a lamb? What strange power did this child use that made her master over her superior?

Strangely, the story of this unusual experience was told to me in the old mill, on the very spot where the uncle took his whipping. Strangely, too, I had devoted nearly a quarter of a century to the study of the power which enabled an ignorant, illiterate child to conquer an intelligent man.

As we stood there in that musty old mill, Mr. Darby

repeated the story of the unusual conquest.

... [Moments later, he] retraced his thirty years of experience as a life insurance salesman, and frankly acknowledged that his success in that field was due, in no small degree, to the lesson he had learned from the child. Mr. Darby pointed out:

"Every time a prospect tried to bow me out, without buying, I saw that child standing there in the old mill, her big eyes glaring in defiance, and I said to myself, 'I've gotta make this sale.' The better portion of all sales I have made, were made after people had said 'NO'."

He recalled, too, his mistake in having stopped only three feet from gold; "but," he said, "that experience was a blessing in disguise. It taught me to keep on keeping on, no matter how hard the going may be, a lesson I needed to learn before I could succeed in anything."'

This story of Mr. Darby and his uncle, the child and the gold mine, doubtless will be read by hundreds of people who make their living by selling life insurance, and to all of these, I wish to offer the suggestion that Darby owes to these two experiences his ability to sell more than a million dollars of life insurance every year.

You can tell a winner by the look in their eyes.

So tell me. And be honest now -

If I were to look deep into your eyes right now, what will I see?

As you go about your day, working hard at whatever it is you're working at, do you do so with an attitude of certainty? With a complete and unquestionable KNOWING that you are on the way to getting exactly what you want, and nothing less; that in fact as far as you're concerned you're already there?

Or do you feel hopeful?

Do you wish?

And try?

Do you give it an earnest crack but keep in mind the possibility that it might not work out?

If you are open to the possibility of failure, then it's failure the world will give you. Success doesn't listen to the call of uncertainty.

Something to Consider

Right now, there is something in your life that you're already a master at. Perhaps it's something as simple as being a gun at packing kid's lunches. More than likely, you have at least one thing in your life that you do effortlessly or at least without really thinking about, that others would LOVE to be master at and yet don't know how.

At the moment I'm doing a heavy lifting phase in my workouts. If you don't know my background, I was a personal trainer for nearly 15 years. I love working out and it's part of my daily routine. Lifting heavy with no rep ranges often goes hand in hand with reasonable rest times between sets, and I was having one such rest yesterday whilst in the middle of my workout. I was sitting on top of the assisted chin up machine, knees folded up against my chest, and just looking around. And for no particular reason the thought crossed my mind -

I wonder what others in the gym see when they look at me.

You see, I see a woman who is still a little out of shape compared with what she'd like to be. (I gave birth to our second child 5 months ago). But I also see a woman - and I hope you can appreciate I say this without meaning to be arrogant! Who is going to be back in bloody brilliant shape before much more time passes? When I glance in the mirror into my eyes while I'm training I see someone who might not be in the best shape in the gym right now, but by God is she training the hardest and by God does she have the most determination.

And I suddenly realised that if only I just applied this same determination and self-belief to areas of my life where I still feel unsure of myself or uncertain of what I can expect to happen, I can truly achieve anything I desire.

Somewhere out there is a woman - thousands of women! - who has no idea how to get back in shape after having a baby and doesn't know if she WILL. And unless she can harness the determination that it will happen and there's no two ways about it, she probably won't.

You take it for granted that you'll succeed in certain areas of your life because you KNOW THAT YOU WILL and you don't question it for a second. But the areas that you take for granted are the ones someone, somewhere, is feeling like a complete failure at, and wondering if they'll ever make it! Meanwhile they or somebody else are KILLING IT at doing something that you'd love to be able to do.

Success has nothing to do with what you know or even with what you've achieved so far. It's ALL what you believe will happen and insist upon MAKING happen.

So what do you believe will happen?

What do you now CHOOSE to make happen?

You can tell a winner by the look in their eyes.

There's not a doubt in my mind that I'll end up back in fantastic shape after having a baby. I can't tell you the exact steps I'll take to get there, as I change my training often and I'm fairly flexible with how I eat. I can't tell you exactly when I'll get there. I certainly can't promise I'll follow all the rules or do everything perfectly until I reach my goal, as there's no way in hell I'm giving up my daily chocolate or subjecting myself to over-analysis about my body. Been there, done that and it's no fun PLUS it doesn't really get me a better result anyway!

But I can tell you that get there I will.

It's simply non-negotiable.

It's time for you to make a non-negotiable choice to make your dreams come true. Make no mistake - if you leave even a shred of doubt in your mind, you'll end up taking it.

You can tell a winner by the look in their eyes.

So stand up. Go to the mirror. And decide, right now, to be a warrior. Decide, right now, that you will NOT fail because you will not QUIT.

Be the determined one.

Be the one who is relentless about attaining her dreams and living with purpose.

Be the one who others look at and are magnetically drawn to because they see success, even long before it's happened.

You can tell a winner by the look in their eyes. It's a look that comes from deep within your soul. And it's a look you absolutely can - and must - cultivate. So make the choice beautiful. Take a stand. And never, EVER forget -

Life is Now. Press Play.

10 Reasons Your Online Business Is Failing

Okay let's be honest - your business? It's not failing. As a matter of fact, it's downright impossible for you to fail at achieving any business - or life - dream so long as you simply refuse to say die.

But sometimes, and often despite your very best effort and analysis, it really does feel as though it's failing.

And that's what I want to talk about today.

The pain that comes with giving your all to a dream you KNOW matters, and having it just not ... quite ... work.

The frustration of pouring your heart and soul to create a new project - whether something relatively simple like a blog post or something really frickin' important and 'bottom line' relevant like an eCourse - and hearing ... well ... crickets.

The heartache of knowing that you really HAVE followed the rules goddamnit, so why isn't it working and why people just can't SEE how great your stuff is and why don't they just go ahead and BUY it already?!

This making money online thang is a tricky beast. Even more so if you insist on making it by doing something you love; something that truly makes your heart sing. In the short-term it can seem easier, even smarter, to just do what you gotta do to get the money rolling in; it can feel as though doing what you REALLY want to do (and succeeding at it) would just be too good to be true.

If right now your business is not working on your terms - if, in fact, you feel as though you're flat out failing and you just don't know how to breakthrough - I'm here to tell you that you CAN 'make it' online, and better still you can do it on your terms.

I've been blessed to have been able to create an incredibly successful online business, in which I make consistent high five figures a month, doing what I love. But I didn't get here on my own; not by any means! I got here because I was fortunate enough to learn from some of the most amazing and inspirational coaches and leaders in the big bad world of www. Some of them I paid. Some of them a lot. Many of them I simply paid attention to. It took me 3 years online before I made a cent, but eventually I found my path. The money was slow at first, and what did come in came mainly from doing what I thought I needed to do for money. Eventually, I found a path where not only could I keep moving forward but on which I could do so ever more - and ever more - on my terms. In the thick of building my business (and let's face it, the evolution never stops!) I failed again and again and again. But the one thing I did do, no matter how far or fast I fell, was pick myself up. A lot of the time, I was able to do that because of the people who helped to PICK me up.

Today, if your business feels as though it SUCKS, I want to pass on the care and support I received so often when I needed it.

Here are 10 reasons your online biz is failing, not quite working yet, and what you need to do about it. Let's call this a mix of the practical how-to and strategy plus the woo-woo inner mindset work. If you want my opinion, the latter matters a whole lot more than the former!

1. Stop pushing. Instead, listen.

First things first. The more you push - try to FORCE - yourself to make things work, the more success will evade you; thumb its nose at you. You were born to succeed by being true to you and by being in alignment. This does not equate to pushing or to desperation. I don't mean you don't have to do the hard work because God knows you gotta put the time and effort in. But when was the last time you really listened in to your intuition about how your business should look, and feel? When was the last time you truly connected with and listened to your clients, and what they want and need? Stop pushing. Start listening. Often you'll find the answers to be a lot more straightforward than what you first thought.

2. What do you really want?

Did you really get into this game so that you could spend hours agonizing over WordPress, social media, or SEO? There are so many (trillions of!) things you could and perhaps 'should' do to build your biz, but none of them come anywhere close to spending daily time providing value by delivering your message. You + speaking your truth + listening to what your peeps want and need + giving it to them = the greatest formula for success even without being an SEO guru and even (gasp!) without a beautiful website. Didn't you once have a simple desire to change people's lives in some way? If you spend an hour every day doing that, and you do so consistently, you'll not only change lives you will change your own. Do ALL the other stuff after that hour (or three) each day.

3. Who are you being?

We all fall into the pattern at times of emulating our coaches or people we look up to online. It's an easy thing to do, especially if you're imitating someone's work who you love. But tell me - can you honestly say that everything about your message and how it's being told is about YOU? Are you being you in your writing or creativity? In your marketing? In your sales approach? You can follow strategy, for SURE. But you gotta bring you into the bargain or it just won't work. And it just won't FEEL good even when it seems to be working.

4. What's the one thing you do?

What is the ONE thing you do in your online biz? You can have a ton of products and offerings. But you have to be able to sum it up with the one thing or you'll confuse yourself and the world. Plus you just won't be in alignment if you're constantly jumping from idea to idea trying to find what works. Stop doing that! Just be you instead! If you look at my business, I have offerings that deal with passion and purpose, with creating your dream body, with building an amazing and profitable business, with living your ideal lifestyle, with being your very best self but if you bring all of that together the 'one thing' I do is I help women like you to create (and live!) their dream life. What's your one thing?

5. Can I tell?

Seriously - if I go to your website, look at your Facebook page, or talk with you - can I tell what your one thing is? If not, chances of me identifying with you and buying anything from you are slim.

6. Are you telling me about it?

What if I don't go visit your site or your page, or decide out of the blue to contact you and ask how you can help me? Is there any way I'm going to KNOW what you do? Osmosis ain't gonna work here, and nor will the collective conscious. You need to be TELLING me about what you do! Tell me about your free stuff, tell me about your paid stuff, and tell me about your crazy high premium stuff! Tell me how you can help me and show me the value you offer and I will love you forever. Don't be afraid to share your gifts! A business mentoring client of mine recently bemoaned how slow her list growth was and it turned out, when I asked, that she wasn't telling people about her free gift at ALL! Surprise, surprise, when she did her list more than doubled in ONE WEEK!

7. Are you inviting me to take action?

It's actually not enough to tell me or even to show me. If

you want me to join your list, download your freebie, or buy your thing you need to tell me in no uncertain terms that that's the next step I should take. You probably need to incentivise me to do it right away as well - I'm a busy and often multi-tasking gal, and I'll plain and simple forget otherwise, even if your thing is the EXACT THING I'M MEANT TO BE DOING. Again - don't be afraid to share your gifts! It's not like you're trying to rip people off, right? We're talking about you creating value to change people's lives. They're not going to get that value and have their life changed if you don't make it very clear how they can do so.

8. Are you giving more than you wanna get?

Speaking of value - and this is so powerful - make it your rule to always give more than you want to receive. If every day you ask yourself what is one simple thing you can do today to provide value? How can you inspire, educate and/or entertain? If you can combine all 3 of those things, or even employ at least one of them, in everything you do then when you do make an offer people will be thrilled to hear from you - and buy from you!

9. Be honest now: are you actually doing what matters?

If you have 2 hours a day, are you working at providing (and delivering) value in that time? Are you making an offer? Or are you working on all the smaller things and even things you THINK are big things but are not in fact at all related to GETTING SH*T OUT THERE AND OFFERING IT TO YOUR

PEEPS and telling yourself that you have to do all that first? If so, you're on a sure-fire track to continued frustration. You can't do everything. You just can't! So you have to get good at doing what counts. KNOW what counts first - for you.

10. You gotta have faith (and a willingness to receive)

This is what it all comes down to. Particularly if you ARE doing all of the above. You can manifest and affirm and do the actual work till the cows come home, but at some point you need to be willing to step back and just receive. And that comes down to faith. Faith - at least in part - supersedes logic. Faith is felt, not counted or 'ticked off'. If you expect things to continue being tough, frustrating, never-ending, they will be. But if you expect your effort to pay off, and you know you're being true to you (and you're actually, you know, providing value in the world) then you WILL succeed. I can't say when, and neither can you. But with faith, the timing doesn't really matter because you KNOW it's going to happen.

I believe in you. I know from my own experience that hard work - especially when it's aligned - DOES pay off. If you refuse to quit, it's impossible to fail. But you sure as heck can get there a lot faster if you implement the above steps!

Remember -

Life is Now. Press Play.

CHAPTER SIX – ONLINE BUSINESS BASIC AND 'MUST-HAVES'

This chapter is very much 'how to' and 'to do', and is based on what I've found to work very well in my nearly 7 years online. Of course most of what I've found to work well has been in the past 3-4 years and so that's what I'll focus on. Bear in mind that everything I share with you here - in fact in this entire book! - is simply my opinion and experience. Of course these are all suggestions that I've tested with great success on my business mentoring clients in my Fearless Wealthy Woman program and not just on myself. But they remain my opinion and experience. The reason I'm pointing this out is simple -

There are a TON of ways to make money online, and a ton of things (depending on whom you listen to) you supposedly 'have' to do. You can't try them all. So if you listen to me, know you are trying MY way - if you're wondering why I don't mention something you've heard of as 'important' (such as SEO to which all I will say is HA), then it's obviously because I don't deem it important based on how I've created success for myself and my clients.

So with that in mind! I've broken this chapter down into 4 key sections:

- Website Basics
- List Building
- Communication Platforms
- Social Media

Let's address them one by one. I encourage you to read this entire chapter and then go back and start implementing. You may prefer to read the book in full before implementing, however you are more likely to get results when you follow through on the advice in each chapter as you go.

Online Business Basics #1: Website Basics

You've heard the expression that 'first impressions count', and nowhere is this more true than in your online home. Just think of how many websites you yourself have flicked past in the past week or month - how many of them do you imagine you stayed on for more than a few seconds? How many for more than a few minutes? Did you stop to remind yourself that this site was likely somebody's pride and joy, and that behind it was a real person with a gift they wanted to share and a desire to create their dream business and life by adding value to YOUR life?

Not likely, right? And nor will other people.

When it comes to standing out and building a raving community of fans online, there is really only one thing that your visitor cares about:

What's in it for me?

That's it.

Your entire job is to show your visitor (and according to research you have less than 0.2% of a second to do that before they decide if your site is 'for them') that you understand them and that you can HELP them. Either that you can help a big problem go away or that you can help them to attain something they really want. So the more bells and whistles and things you add because you think they look pretty or might be of interest, the more you actually detract from your core message.

Remind me - (and you!) - what IS your core message again? What is your business all about? If you can't answer that really quickly then go back to the previous chapter and repeat the exercises!

As you go through the rest of this book I want you to keep

this idea in back of your mind:

The more I can remind my clients/website visitors of how I can add value to their lives and HELP them, the faster my business will flourish!

Okay then. Let's talk about what should be on your website. I'm no WordPress (or any sort of tech/'site building) expert so that's not what this is about. I'm talking purely from a functionality point of view for getting customers and making money!

You need:

- A clear and clean layout. Think 'less is more'. Don't try and make sure people know about ALL your stuff and all your ideas on the home page. You'll just confuse them, and they'll leave. Each page should have one - ONE - main purpose.

- A way for people to 'opt in' to receive your emails and/or newsletter. Typically this appears top right on the website, for the reason that most people's eyes go top right first. Your opt in should be easily visible (think big enough!) and pleasing to the eye. Usually you will offer something in exchange for people's email address, i.e. a free download, report, video or other sort of gift. Your freebie MUST be of high value to your audience - if they don't receive value with your free gift, why would they buy your paid product or service?! Your free opt in will be connected to an email responder service such as

AWeber, Mailchimp or Infusionsoft. I recommend AWeber for start-up and small businesses. I used it for the first 6 years in my business, and only switched to the pricier Infusionsoft when my list was over 10k.

- An 'About' page, which should definitely inform visitors about who you are but first it should speak to your reader. It's ACTUALLY about them, not you! So I encourage you to open with something that speaks straight to the core of why your reader is there and what they most need right now. From there you might go in to your story and about you, and then finish with your professional bio. Include 1-3 testimonials in your 'about' page if possible, as well as reminders to opt in for your free newsletter and gift. For an example, visit www.katloterzo.com/about

- A 'Work With Me' page, which links to any coaching you may offer and/or products and services. You don't have to call it 'Work With Me'. It could be 'Coaching', or 'Products', or 'Books'. Whatever is relevant and right. You might even have a few of those pages i.e. 'Coaching' and 'Books'. There's no wrong or right, just bear in mind that the less options you give people on your site the more it is clear what you most want them to do.

- A 'Contact' page. If you encourage communication, have this on the top navigation bar of your site. If you prefer not to encourage a lot of emails, have a small link to it in the footer.

- A 'Blog' page, unless your homepage is your blog (which it often is), but even then you should still have a link back to it.

- Other pages you might consider are resources, shop or store (usually for physical items), a direct link to your signature program if/when you have one.

Questions to ask yourself:

What is the #1 purpose of your site? For example, it might be to collect leads. Usually that will be the #1 goal!

What is the #2 goal of your site? I.e. for me, I want people to read my blog posts and start to be 'drawn in' to what I write and see themselves in the writing. My reasoning is that when people relate to me they will want to know more from me, and become a truly active member of my community.

What sort of colours do you like?

What is the 'feel' you want to bring across?

What are 3 websites you love the look and feel of?

And 3 that you can't stand?

All of this helps you to become clear on what your site should be about, and will also help you brief a designer should you decide to use one. It is much smarter to decide all of these things in advance, rather than try and figure them out on the fly! Remember you can always change your mind as you go.

Online Business Basics #2: List Building

There are 3 primary areas you need to consider when it comes to building your list, and thus your ability to be profitable and help a lot of people. As an aside, it's certainly possible to make a lot of money with a small list (typically through phone sales or live events) but the expression 'the money is in the list' really does hold true for most of us!

The 3 areas are:

- Generating leads
- Capturing leads
- Keeping leads

Let's go through them one by one.

Generating Leads

When all is said and done, generating new leads for your business is not at all about what clever tricks you might be able to come up with or learn from the 'internet marketing powers that be'. Sure, sometimes you'll come across a strategy for new and fast growth, but more often than not the best way to generate new leads for your business is, quite simply, to provide valuable content, and plenty of it. The more great content you create, the more you will build your brand. The more FREE great content you send out into the world, the faster still you will build your brand and establish yourself as an expert in your field. You should aim always for your content to in some way educate, inspire or entertain (or all 3!) your audience. If you can do this well, and often, you'll find people sharing your stuff and your traffic will naturally grow.

Now. Allow me to be perfectly clear - I do NOT mean 'build it and they will come'. You definitely still need to market and actively do what you can to get your work out there. I'm quite sure that there are literally hundreds of thousands, if not millions of websites and blogs that have good or even great content on them but no more than a handful of people know about it.

My point is this - I see so many people who want to 'make it' online getting very caught up in what sort of internet marketing knowledge they need to have and doing so at the expense of just being really freaking awesome and helpful to their community. Content is king, and everything else comes AFTER that. The best sales and marketing strategies in the world won't help you if your stuff isn't helping others.

That being said, some of the best ways to generate new leads and the ones I've had great results with:

- Writing insanely useful, inspiring and/or entertaining blog posts and getting them shared on social media. List posts work very well, but any great post can do the trick. Pay attention to good formatting and use a great image as well as appropriate keywords and categories.

- Guest posting IF it is done on sites that are relevant to your audience and themselves have a reasonable amount of traffic. Don't expect to be accepted on the big sites straightaway though! Maybe you will, but you probably will need to cut your teeth on sites that match your own audience and experience. Creating high value freebies, such as a free report, webinar or training event, video/audio or video/audio series, mini eBooks and so on. Drive traffic to these freebies using your own audience (asking for shares can do wonders!) as well as social media advertising. At the time of writing this, Facebook advertising is one of the most effective and low-cost ways to generate new leads. It's outside of the scope of this book to try and teach Facebook advertising (it needs its own book and it would also need frequent updating, whereas the strategies I'm teaching in this book are for the most part timeless).

- You can find any number of free resources on Facebook advertising online but if you want to learn it in detail and have the latest updated information as well as my personal input into creating successful ads for your business, consider applying for a free

Business Strategy Session with me at www.katloterzo.com/application. Note these sessions are only given to women who are serious about building an online business and willing to be 'fearless' in doing so.

- Being active on social media - choose 1-2 social media platforms that work well for your audience, and stick with them; don't try and be everywhere. Learn about your chosen platform and track your growth as well as engagement

- Add social media share and like buttons to your blog posts

Kat's pick: the most effective of all these strategies is to create high-value freebies and do whatever is needed to drive traffic to the opt in page. As mentioned, at the time of writing, the best way to do this is Facebook advertising as well as asking your audience to share your freebie.

Capturing Leads

It's all very well to generate new traffic, using the strategies just described, but if you don't actually 'capture' those leads (meaning their email addresses) then the whole thing is fairly pointless! Here are my tips on making sure people want to join your email list and online community:

Remember that leads are people. They aren't faceless, nameless wallets walking around just anxious to join your list and buy your stuff. It's easy to get caught up in talking about your list and growing your database but if you can stop daily to remind yourself that you're talking about real people, often similar people to you since they're in your niche, who have their own hopes and dreams and then ask yourself how you can HELP them today, that's when you will forge true connections and grow a community of people who actually love you and will be loyal to you for life. Anyone can grow a list. Having a great relationship with that list takes work, but it will ensure you not only KEEP your list but also that you get the sort of satisfaction out of your business that you went into it hoping for.

- Make it simple. NEVER assume people know what to do. People spend less than a second flicking past your message, so if you don't do something to grab their attention you won't GET their attention. If you have a free opt in created then be very clear and obvious about where and how they should sign up. TELL them exactly what to do even to the extent of saying 'Put your email in the box below now'. Yes, they can see for themselves that there is an email sign up box there. But yes you will get higher conversions if you actually tell them to use it - and use the word 'now'!

- Give your best stuff away for free. I'm not talking about all of your secrets and every detail of your strategy. But don't make your free stuff sub-par, or nobody will want to buy your paid stuff. The rule is that the more great content you give away for free, the more people want to be part of your community and the greater eventual return you'll receive on that free content.

- Remind people. Don't assume that just because you told people once, they remember. People are busy! Why on earth should they REMEMBER to sign up to your free thing or indeed do anything? Perhaps it caught their eye on Facebook but then they got distracted. The message here is be as visible as possible. The more people see your name, face and offers around the more they start to wonder who you are and whether they shouldn't check you out.

- Stand out. Bring the uniqueness of 'you' to all that you do, whether it's the name of your freebie, the colours and style you use, how you talk on social media or (ideally) all of it. Don't be just another bland and boring fitness or wellness guru, or coach, or business consultant. The more you can bring YOU to all that you do, the more memorable you'll be and the more you'll find your tribe.

Kat's pick: Be you!

Keeping Leads

If you want to develop a long-term relationship with your list and build a truly loyal and engaged community who cannot WAIT until you release something new, then you need to know and understand what your audience want and need. You need to know how to educate, inspire and entertain them and most of all you need to be able to deeply CONNECT with them.

The most effective way to do all of this is to be true to you. The more you 'try' to be deliberately helpful, inspiring or entertaining the more you risk losing your true voice and becoming somewhat dry and blah. Sure, it's good to think about what your audience most want and need and to brainstorm on different ideas for articles you might write, freebies you might create, or products you might launch, but when you go to actually CREATE - be you, the creator. You already know everything you need to know. I can tell you without a shadow of a doubt that unless your audience is in fact made up of research analysts who only want research based analysis, then researching a blog post or article will result in a boring piece that falls flat. It's NOT about what you can teach, it's about your perspective on what you can teach.

So rant. Be honest. Say what you really think, even if you're terrified to hit publish. Be the message and gift you wish YOU had a few years ago.

Here are some other tips:

- Constantly ask yourself - how can I help? How can I be of service? The answer to these questions doesn't matter at all; the point is simply to ask and therefore remind yourself that if you want to be loved and appreciated you must first love and appreciate.

- The more you give, the more you get. Which I kind of already said, but seriously. True stuff.

- Pay attention to which audiences YOU remain a part of. What is it about them that keeps your attention, compared with the ones you unsubscribe from?

- Give at least 3x as much free content/value as how much you sell. An interesting point on this is that it is entirely possible to sell AND give value at the same time. So you don't necessarily have to, for example, send out 3 different freebie based emails before you can offer something for sale. What if you included free value in your sales PROCESS in the first place? Some of the really big name internet marketers, such as Frank Kern, do this extremely well

- Be useful. It's not about you, it's about them. Nobody wants to hear about the epiphany you had on your holiday or whilst doing yoga unless it is directly related back to them.

Kat's pick: Be insanely you and be insanely useful. Every. Damn. Day.

Online Business Basics #3: Communication Platforms

The beauty of running an online business is that there's no

shortage of ways for you to connect with your audience, increase your traffic, grow your list and ultimately build that biz. Below are the ones worth paying attention to. You don't have to do them all. You're far better off to decide which 1 or 2 platforms are right for you and to do them really damn well rather than try and spread yourself too thin and be a master of all trades. It makes sense to choose the platform that you're most drawn to! Don't you dare try and do something that you internally resist just because you've heard or seen that others are kicking butt at it. I can promise you it either just won't work ('cause you won't be GREAT at it if your heart's not in it) or else you'll plain old quit. So either way, it just won't work.

Repeat after me: be you. be you. be you. be YOU!

Written blogs: blogging is the 'old school' way of building your business and community online. I'm talking of course about written blogs, which is the original way to blog. Every website should have a blog, however it could be written, audio or video (or a combo). Unless you enjoy writing and can do it well I don't recommend trying to push out written posts. People's attention spans are short and they'll feel it if you battled to write a post as opposed to if it flowed naturally and authentically. It will also take YOU a lot of time and cause a fair deal of frustration doing something that doesn't come naturally to you. YES you can learn and perhaps you should. But consider first if there's not another way that might serve you and your community just as well, if not better. Something worth bearing in mind is that building your business successfully doesn't have to be hard work in the sense that it doesn't have to go against your grain. So many people have told me they can't be as successful as me because they can't write but writing has nothing to do with my success. It's just the tool I've used! My success is based on my determination and refusal to NOT succeed, and yours will be based on the same unbreakable foundation.

Regardless of which form of blogging is right for you, I recommend that you DO blog. It's one of the most valuable ways of sharing your message with your audience, giving people a chance to relate to and connect with you, and showing that you can help. It's also one of the most indirect ways of effective selling, for example by 'seeding' links to your product and by drawing a natural connection between your product and the problem/solution your blog posts talks about. I recommend blogging at least once a month. If you enjoy it and you are also regularly sending out free opt in-based content to grow your list then I recommend blogging as often as once a week. It really can be a very powerful tool.

Audio blogs or podcasts. All of the above applies to audio blogs as well. One thing to consider is what your audience prefers, if you're not sure which form of blogging feels right for you. Of course there's also nothing to stop you doing a mix of all types and working out your most effective option as you go! If you choose to do audio based blog or podcast, then I recommend you do so at least somewhat 'off the cuff'. Writing a script out will take a lot of time but more importantly, it will cause you to come across as stilted and rehearsed rather than authentic. Length is really up to you - if the content is valuable you can go as long as you like! Over 40 minutes is quite rare and you'd want to be sure you will maintain people's interest if you do choose to go that long. I've recorded podcasts as short as a few minutes long. A good length seems to be 6-10 minutes, if it's just a quick audio blog - if it's something more in-depth or educational than 20-40 minutes is about the norm. The easiest way to make an audio blog or podcast is to record straight into your computer. If you use a Mac, as I do, then there is a free inbuilt recorder called Quicktime Player. It allows you to do audio, video or even to screencast if you wanted to make a slide-based video presentation.

Video blogs. Exactly the same feedback as I just gave you for audio, however you will also need to consider appearance if you're doing a video of yourself. I definitely do NOT mean you need to 'pretty yourself up'. If you want to do 'fancy' hair and makeup and get all of your lighting sorted, that's awesome and you'll definitely have more polished and beautiful videos to show for it. But you do not HAVE to have that stuff to get started. I was recording videos on my iPhone for over 3 years before I started worrying about that sort of thing, and even now all I do is put a dash of foundation and makeup on - my 'trick' is I always film outdoors in a sunny location so I don't have to worry about lighting! But I used to do videos in my kitchen, my lounge, anywhere - just using the reverse camera feature on my phone. Some of the videos looked pretty awful! But they did the job and that's the main thing. My point is simple:

regardless of what the task in your business is, start now and correct later. Videos can be as short as 90 seconds (I wouldn't go shorter) and really shouldn't be over 8-10 minutes unless they are instructional. If educative they might go for as long as an hour, or even more.

Remember that regardless of which form of blogging you decide to start with, you can always change your mind as you go, or indeed at any time! Just be consistent, even if consistent means only once a month. And for the love of God - once you've written a blog tell people about it! Send out an email to your peeps, and post it on all your networks. Don't be afraid to ask people to 'share if they enjoyed'. People will NOT do this out of the goodness of their hearts unless the post was truly life-changing, but they won't hesitate to do it if you request it.

Social media. For a good many years I battled to figure out a way to make my presence well known across all social media platforms. I felt awful about the fact that although I had a pretty good Facebook following (over 23k on my initial business page) my profiles on Twitter, Google+, Pinterest, Instagram and LinkedIn were like a ghost town. Sometimes I still try and tell myself I need to get it together and be visible everywhere and then I slap myself in the face and remind myself I built my business to over 50k a month in income withOUT being visible in all those places. Don't get me wrong - I'm sure that being well-known across all of social media would be a BIG help in growing my brand AND it would increase my income. But at what cost? It already takes me upwards of 30 minutes a day to maintain a great

Facebook presence, and my time is precious. If I were to invest similar time into even 3 more platforms that would end up being all that I do, INSTEAD of writing this and my other books! I spend around 4 hours a day, 5 days a week on my business - with 2 young children and my lifestyle and sanity to maintain (by choice!) - that's all I am willing to do. So there's no way I'm going to spend half that time each day on social media. For me, my writing always comes first and must take the majority of my available time.

What comes first for you? Do that most of the time, spend half of the extra time you have planning and administrating your business and the remainder on lead generation, marketing and sales processes, and I promise, everything else will take care of itself. It's a rough guide, but one I've found to work very well.

Guest blogging or interviews. Guest blogging truly deserves its own category as a communication platform. Done well, it can be the difference between your message disappearing into the nether-regions of the internet and becoming 'famous' as a blogger and a brand. Here's the hard truth: just because you have an important message to share and kick BUTT as a writer does NOT mean people will find you, and even if they find you they're not going to care enough to share your stuff with their friends or on their blogs. One of the smartest ways to make your presence known online is to be a guest blogger on popular sites. I will say that this is no longer something you can just have at the click of your fingers. You need to be good, you need to be interesting, you need to stand out from the often hundreds of submissions big-name bloggers receive DAILY, and of course you need to be super relevant to their audience.

Online Business Basics #4: Social Media

We've touched on this briefly, but it really needs its own area.

Let's face it: social media is pretty much impossible to ignore as a critical part of your business. For traffic growth, engagement, and low-cost advertising purposes you really can't beat it. Hopefully you enjoy connecting with your true fans and finding new ones through social media, but therein lies the 'rub' - if you DO love social media it can be easy to end up spending WAY too much time on it. Have you ever found yourself scrolling repeatedly through your Facebook newsfeed as though looking for the meaning of life? I know I have - it's a serious addiction at times! And if you don't really love social media, then guess what? Too bad. You will seriously reduce your business growth abilities if you don't use it, and that's going to affect your bottom line. The long and short of it is that you must have some sort of social media presence. That being said, you don't have to be everywhere all at once. I spent several years trying to motivate myself to be 'properly' active on Pinterest, Instagram and Twitter and just kept resisting it. I like Facebook. I find it easy. It feels natural. And so that's where I'm active, and that's where I've built an (over 25k total between my pages) fan base. Finally I decided to just 'quit' the idea of having to be great or even good at all social media platforms. To be honest, I did this because I read advice from other successful entrepreneurs recommending that you should just do one really well rather than spread yourself thin and have a half-hearted go at too many platforms. I like that idea!

Here are my recommendations for your effective social media presence:

- Where is your audience? Choose one (maybe two) social media platforms that you want to master. Even if you have 8-10 hours a day available to work on your business, you should spend most of that time creating content/projects and setting up marketing and sales. Most (although not all) of which does NOT mean 'hanging out' on social media. Unless your business IS to hang out on social media, I recommend maximum one hour a day spent on it. Personally I try to limit it to half an hour, as my preferred work time each day adds up to no more than 4 hours, 5 days a week. It makes sense to choose the social media platforms that you personally enjoy and that your audience also enjoys. Hopefully there is a match there!

- Be structured. Don't hop on and off social media all day. It's a massive time waster and I promise you that a day spent on social media is NOT one that's going to have you going to bed at night feeling so awesome about how 'in flow' you were for the day. Set aside 1-2 blocks of time where you go and schedule posts, answer comments etc. Personal social media time might be separate but still not the greatest use of your time and certainly not 'true' relaxation in my opinion!

- Use the 3:4 value to sell ratio: this is a must whether we're talking sending emails or social media updates. Of course you want to tell people about what you have for them, and assuming your offerings match your niche's needs they're also going to want to hear about it! But you can't sell more than what you provide value. Aim to provide value (free) at least 75% of the time, and sell approximately 25% of the time. You can 'get away with' more sales and marketing if it also provides value at the same time.

- Use the WIIFM principle. 'What's in it for me' is what that means; 'me' being your reader, not you. People want to be educated, inspired, and entertained. How can you do that today? Ask yourself every day and make an effort to provide that for people and your social media efforts will pay off. Include some personal information from time to time, so people can get a sense of who you are. Photos of what you're up to in your free time or even from where you're working are a great idea for this.

- Be real. Avoid copying what others are doing on social media and definitely avoid trying to come up with posts you think will get high engagement and likes. By all means THINK about it, but what I mean is - be you. Be authentic. Talk in your own voice. After all, the whole idea is to find customers who love the real you, right?

Before You Leave This Chapter!

Go back through the suggestions for each section in this chapter on Online Business Basics, and make yourself a 5-point list of what you will take action on this week. Please don't choose more than 5 points! Schedule them in your diary and then get out and actually TAKE that action this week!

CHAPTER SEVEN – CREATING YOUR MONEY PLAN

Eeek! This is the exciting part where you start to actually bring it all together! If you're thinking you don't yet feel ready to start charging money for your services or launch your first online product, can I politely remind you to shut that voice of madness down? Bitch-slap it if you have to! After all, the whole purpose of your online business is that it is a BUSINESS, right? Not a hobby. Not a charity. A business. And businesses make money. Also - here's something that I managed to take 3 years to realise in my own business and that I want you to really take to heart NOW.

If you don't offer anything for sale, you won't sell anything!

I know. It is a SHOCKER. In all seriousness, though - I spent 3, nearly 4 years too scared, shy, and overwhelmed to actually create anything and offer it to my audience. In my defence, I joined the online world to be a writer and build a blog, and only really thought about the business side of it later; once I really realised the potential. But still. Craziness.

Before you read any further, I want you to promise me that you will commit to launching (or re-launching) at least one offering this month, as a result of reading this chapter. If you don't yet have an online business to launch something FROM, no problem. Go back to the website basics chapter. Buy a domain name. Get somebody to set up your site (you can hire someone for $5 on www.fiverr.com). And launch that business. Launch your first product as well! Who cares if you have 5 people on your list, and 4 live with you? The point is you are taking action and saying 'yes' to building your business even before you are 'ready'.

(I'll tell you a secret ... shhh ... you'll NEVER be ready!)

So. Let's talk money. What I'm about to share with you represents the exact processes I've used to grow an online business that made me 5, 10, 20, 30 and then over 50k per month in income. These are also processes I use (obviously in a lot more detail!) with my personal mentoring clients.

Product and Offering Options

There are no doubt a million and one ways that you could make money online. I haven't tried them all, and I daresay I never will. So I'm not going to try and teach them all to you. Instead, I'm going to share what I know and what I have found to work for me and for my clients.

1:1 coaching or consulting - you charge an hourly rate to work with clients over phone or Skype (for example). Typically this does NOT include you doing anything for them, nor should it include giving them access to your strategies, tools etc. It is a trade of your time for money. You can literally charge whatever you like for this. Have a look at what others in your niche are charging, but don't be afraid to go higher if you believe your services are of greater value in some way or just because you are YOU!

1: many coaching - exactly the same, but to a group. This might be a small group or it could be huge; there are no rules. Price will obviously be less than 1:1, and the more people in the group typically the lower the price each individual would pay.

eBooks - an eBook can be created in as little as a day, depending on the length. When it comes to length less is definitely MORE. People are busy and just won't read the whole thing if it's too long. In all honesty, whilst I recommend having one or two eBooks in your product 'funnel' so that you can catch people with a lower end sale, they are way more trouble than they're worth. In some ways creating an eBook takes more time and energy than creating an entire online program, and it will typically sell for as low as 10% of the cost! Depending on what's in your eBook the price could, in theory, be as high as you like (i.e. a one page eBook that shows me how to make a million dollars might be worth thousands!) but in reality people don't expect to pay more than about $30 or $40 for an eBook. You can increase the price upwards of $50 if you include bonus reports, giveaways, and audios and so on. My most successful eBook is my Look Great Naked Eating Plan, which I sell for $57 including 8 bonuses. There is no rule on how long or short an eBook should be. Personally I feel under 50 pages works well, but it depends on your topic. I have one eBook that is really a full on 'book' book and is 246 pages. It was my first eBook and I truly tried to share EVERYTHING I knew about my topic. It's a great book and those who read it all the way through will benefit greatly. My concern is how many people DO read it all the way through, and also whether they implement what they learned. In some ways people will get better results from accessing the same information via a weekly eCourse or membership, as they are being told what to do each week. The bonus for you is, you can repurpose your eBook information (adding more detail of course) into an eCourse and charge hundreds or even thousands more and know that your audience are in turn receiving that value!

eCourses/Online Boot Camps - these are definitely the way to go, and absolutely where they money is at. Having a signature program is something that I believe every woman in business simply MUST do. You might have more than one signature program, and that's fine. I have 3, ranging in price from $199 to several thousand. A high value eCourse can go as high as $20,000 in price. Again, look at what others in your niche are doing, but don't be afraid to step out of the box and do your own thing. An eCourse typically runs over a period of weeks - 4-8 seems to be average, but it could be as low as 3 weeks and it could go for as much as 3 months. Anything longer than that and it would really be called a -

Membership - Similar to an eCourse, however it tends to be longer; even up to 12 months. I don't think programs that run more than 4 months are worth it, and I've spoken to many other entrepreneurs who feel the same way. The reason is that no matter how awesome your content, people just start dropping off after 4 months! When I launched my 'Woman Incredible VIP Platinum Mentoring' (a 12 month program) in 2011, I was DEVASTATED at the drop off rate in engagement after the 4-month mark. I truly thought I'd created an amazing and life-changing program that my audience needed, and I was so upset to think that maybe my program just sucked! So it was a huge relief when I learned that this is just normal. People move on. And let's face it - creating a 12-month program kinda blows!

Both eCourses and memberships typically contain a mixture of content including written and usually some form of audio or video. Typically the more multimedia you use, the more you can charge. It's also smart to use different forms of teaching as people learn in different ways, plus it rounds the program out. You would usually include something like a Facebook or other sort of forum, and possibly live Q&A and/or coaching webinars or calls with you personally (in a group format). Depending on the price of your eCourse, and what you want to do, you may or may not be actively involved in the Facebook group.

Mastermind - a mastermind is sort of similar to an eCourse or membership in that it typically contains weekly training comprising a mix of written, video and audio. The big difference is that a mastermind costs a lot more, and in return you give a lot more of your time. This might mean regular Q&A/coaching calls, your time in the forum and even 1:1 time. A mastermind is usually a small group of select clients (possibly application only) who you will work with intensively to get a desired result. It's kind of like combining 1:1 coaching with access to all of your strategy, resources and tools. My business mastermind, 'Fearless Wealthy Woman', for example, runs over 8 weeks and gives my clients extreme access to me as well as access to all of my knowledge, skills, resources, strategies and tools - things I have literally spent 7 years and paid hundreds of thousands of dollars to learn.

Webinars/Coaching Calls: paid or free. Webinars and coaching calls or teleclasses are one of the most effective and low-cost ways to grow your 'list' or community as well as to provide high-value free content which can very naturally lead into a sale. I recommend you do NOT wait until you feel 'ready' to host a webinar, or even until you have a big list. Just jump straight in and run one now. I've found it well worth my while to host one a month. I choose topics based on what I'm interested in as well as what my audience wants and needs - the more you can match your own passions with the immediate 'must haves' of your audience, the more sign-ups, as well as, live attendees you'll have! It is pretty scary the first time you run a webinar but once you do you'll realise it's just like talking on the phone. Give yourself permission to just be YOU - mistakes, fumbles and all. Nobody wants to listen to a robot. If you want to make it really easy on yourself, start with teleclasses and no slides. Once you feel ready to up level you can move to a slide-based presentation. I use Instant Teleseminar to host all my webinars and teleclasses. Typically you will want to give people around 2-3 weeks notice, and be sure to send them reminder emails in the lead up as well as on the day. You can use your webinars/teleclasses simply as free value-packed offers (make sure you record them as well for future giveaways!) or you can use them as a natural way to lead into a sales presentation of one of your products or programs, and even offer a special discount for webinar listeners only.

Physical products: I haven't experimented a great deal with selling physical products, although I do have my own protein powder line for women, which has sold several hundred thousand dollars' worth over the past 2 or 3 years. To be honest I've been very lucky with that - I didn't have to spend much time or effort marketing it. I'd already invested that time and energy in creating my online community of women and providing them so much great free content on fitness and fat loss, that when I launched the protein powder; something that most gym-going women purchase anyway, it was an easy choice for many of my audience to buy it. Especially since it's organic, tastes amazing (unlike most proteins) and sells for less than half the price of similar quality products. Sorry ... couldn't help myself there with a tiny pitch! If you do decide to launch a physical product my recommendation firstly is do NOT do so just for the money unless you can do so with relatively low start-up costs and time input. If your PASSION is to launch a physical product, that's different. Know that for the most part it will take a fair deal of time and money to get it off the ground, as well as possibly in-depth research and trial and error. If there's something you can introduce simply as an arm of your business, that matches what you're already doing, like I did with my protein powder that would certainly be a great starting point. I was fortunate to have a friend who already owned a protein powder company, so I didn't have to do any research, but I will say it would have been worth my while to do so had I not had that connection.

Live or Online Events: a FANTASTIC way to boost your cash flow, as well as bring new clients into your business. I love to run live events but they are extremely energy-demanding and time-consuming, so it's certainly not something I'd want to do regularly. Unless your goal is to build a business around speaking, you probably won't either. That being said, running an event - whether an evening workshop, a full day event, or even a 2 or 3 day event- is one of the most effective ways to boost your income. This is particularly true if you don't do it often, as people will jump on the chance to work with you 'live'. Face to face events are great of course, but you can also host (paid) online workshops. During my pregnancy last year I hosted a paid 3-hour event for women wanting to grow their business, and I did it all online. This was great for me as I was heavily pregnant, but it was also great for my attendees as they could listen in from anywhere in the world! If you decide to run a live event, be sure to allow at least one month's notice. You can use your events purely as a product in themselves, or (and this is what I'd recommend) you can use them to lead in to selling a higher priced product. For example, you might host an evening event for a very low price, and at that event 'upsell' your more expensive full day or 2-day program. You could then upsell a membership or mastermind program at the end of that 2-day event. Always be thinking of ways you can add value to your community - which means always ask yourself 'what's the next thing my customers will need?' Don't fall into the trap of thinking you 'shouldn't' keep selling. People want you to sell if what you are selling is something that will help solve their problems or get them to their goals!

Testing your products and services

Here is the MOST important thing to know about going live with your products, programs, events, services and offerings - Never, ever, ever, EVER fully create it until you've sold it.

Sounds weird, right? But here's what I mean. Imagine you have this FANTASTIC idea for a program or product or an event, and you just KNOW it is going to kick butt and people everywhere are going to be signing up for it in droves. Especially with the awesome deal you're going to offer them!

I hate to be a bubble burster, but it just doesn't really work like that. Or at least not until you have some level of 'fame' whereby at least a portion of your community will pretty much buy anything you do, without even looking at the price or what they're getting! That might sound really strange, but think about it - isn't there at least one person you follow online, who, were they to suddenly offer a special 'one-off' event or opportunity to work with them you'd be pulling out your credit card before you even checked all the details? Maybe that's just how I think about some of my favourite online muses :) but I don't think it's just me. And certainly that's the goal for all of us; to be 'that person' but for now, let's step back down to the real world.

Imagine you took your awesome idea, and you made sure you were TOTALLY organised before announcing it. This means you spent:

- Money
- Time
- Energy
- Emotion

And no doubt pulled out a lot of hair in the process.

(Not to mention other areas of your business/life had to take a hit for a while, as you can't do everything all at once!)

Finally, you're ready! With excitement and pride, you write up an email announcement or perhaps host a live webinar or teleclass to let people know about it. You sit back, and wait for the sales to come in. And what you get is ... nothing. Or perhaps one or two sign ups. Maybe an email inquiry. And you truly don't get it, you put your heart and soul into this creation and even included a fantastic early bird sign up offer. So why aren't people joining?!

I have a simple answer for you -

You never stopped to ask them if that's what they wanted.

Of course the goal for all of us is to be completely tuned in with what our niche want and desire. In theory we should be so 'inside their minds' that we just can't go wrong. But the reality is that EVERYTHING must be tested, and it doesn't matter how long you've been in business it's still possible to have your ideas flop. As a matter of fact, the more ideas you're trialling and getting out there, the more likely you are to have some of them flop! It's just how it goes, and the goal is not to STOP that failure. For every bad idea you thought was so great, you're one step closer to the freaking awesome idea that takes off like wildfire.

But for the love of God, don't go ahead and create things - or spend significant time or money on them - until you know that people WANT them!

When it comes to testing, here's what to ask yourself. Go through this mini-checklist each time you come up with an idea that you want to have a crack at going ahead with:

Who will buy it? Write out a 'profile' on the ideal customer for this product or idea. It could be that profile exactly matches the profile of your niche. But write it out anyway. Usually each product or service you offer will appeal to a 'niche within your niche', i.e. there may be specific issues this ideal client has right NOW that you haven't included in your overall niche description.

How do you know? Seriously - how do you know they will buy it? What makes you so sure? Have you ASKED anyone? You don't have to email your list and ask 'please will you buy my thing' :) but it doesn't hurt to test the waters. Before I launched my Look Great Naked Online Bootcamp back in 2012 (a program which made me over $70,000 in a 6-month period and officially put me in the ranks of 'woman who makes money online'!) I asked my audience, just on Facebook, if they thought it was a good idea. I wish I had kept that post! But basically what I said was 'I'm thinking of running a 6 or 8 week bikini body program or 'Bootcamp'. What do you think? Would this be something you'd like? I'd probably include meal plans, training programs (for home or gym), motivation and mindset work, recipes, live coaching calls and a forum. Let me know if this sounds like something you need, also if there's anything I've left out!'

Can you see how simple and easy that is to do? And not only do you get immediate feedback, as well as the chance to hear if there's anything you haven't considered, but you also have the chance to 'tease' people with the idea that your program is coming. This is what's called a 'pre-launch', albeit a very informal one! And it's very effective. Launching a program that nobody knew is coming is not really a great idea! We'll talk more about sales later.

How can you improve it? When you ask people for their feedback, really listen. It doesn't mean you have to take it all on! Recently I had someone give feedback that she'd like me to create FODMAP food plans. This is a specific approach to nutrition based on a fairly rare condition that I don't actually fully understand. So obviously I'm not going to do it; it's not my area of genius. But often people in your audience will make suggestions you never thought of yourself. In fact, that's where my Look Great Naked Eating Plan came from - I had launched my 12-month VIP Platinum Membership and it was doing quite well. One of my members asked me if I could just write up a complete list of all 'allowed' foods and all that were best to avoid, so I happily obliged. But what started out as a simple list ended up turning into a 57-page eBook with 8 bonuses, and one that has made me multiple 5-figures since then!

How can you monetise it risk free? Do everything you can to avoid spending money on your new idea until it is MAKING money. Look, sometimes you have to suck it up and put some money down. Clearly you need a website, checkout buttons (free through PayPal, mind you) and so on. But here's what you do NOT need in order to go live with a program or product:

A website you have paid top $$ to have beautified. Pretty website does not equal higher income. There are some damn ugly sites out there that make great money and some truly stunning ones that do NOT. Your program will sell if it gets results not if it looks nice.

Copywriting. Figure it out yourself for now.

Graphic designer stuff i.e. logos, pretty PDFs. MAKE DO.

Fancy video creation or editing. MAKE DO. Use your iPhone with a nice background such as in a park or at the beach!

Spending money on ad campaigns straight to your product. People opt in for FREEBIES from an ad campaign, it is much harder to sell something straight off an ad. Get them in with your freebie, and then upsell gradually after first giving quality free content.

The basic message here is that you can absolutely bootstrap it with your first products and services and you SHOULD. Personally I didn't pay a single designer to work on my website until my income was over 30k per MONTH. I know people who've spent as much as 60k getting a website ready and then their program didn't work! Even 5k wasted is too much; heck even $50 WASTED is too much. And it's just not necessary. If you're telling yourself you first have to have 'x' before you can launch, you're simply procrastinating out of fear and self-doubt. Get over it!

Before You Leave This Chapter!

What is your biggest 'aha' moment from this chapter? Write it down. And then -

Out of the options I've given you for 'money makers' what would you most LOVE to do?

What would be easiest/simplest for you to do right away?

What would that involve or include?

When will you have it go 'live' (set a date even if you think you'll end up changing it! Just commit)

Create a simple plan for how you're going to test that offer - and do it!

Now move on to learn about marketing and then sales :)

CHAPTER EIGHT - MARKETING

The next thing we need to look at in creating your money plan is your marketing. And this definitely deserves its own chapter! Initially I was going to include marketing and sales in the previous chapter, but let's face it - failing to invest proper attention into how you actually get your stuff out there and into people's hands means that you WON'T. Which in turn means no money for you. Clearly there's no point having the best products and programs if you're not also marketing to your peeps about it! For me, I like to think of marketing simply as making sure people know. There is a lot of negative association with sales and marketing. Many people - perhaps you - feel like the whole thing must be 'icky' or that sales people are all sleazy. I once worked with a coach who INSISTED that selling is love, and while it sounds a bit corny I have to say I agree.

Here's a simple way to look at it:

Are you creating something that's high value that you have designed to help people get rid of a pain or achieve a goal? Yes? Good!

Are you deliberately setting out to manipulate people and rid them of their money just so you can 'get rich quick'? No? Of course not, right?

You're creating something that will HELP people. To solve PROBLEMS that they actually have or to get them to a goal that they truly long to attain. Am I right? So with that in mind, why in God's good name are you telling yourself it's wrong to sell or market the damn thing? How is it going to actually help people if you don't let them know about it? And wouldn't YOU want to hear about a product or program that could truly help you?!

Okay then :)

Here are the things I've found crucial to consider when it comes to your marketing, and an overview of how to approach each in your business:

Pre-launch

Your pre-launch is the period of time (usually 1-3 weeks) before your offer goes live and is open for sign-ups or registrations. The purpose of your pre-launch is:

Make people aware your offer is coming

Arouse interest/anticipation

Garner any feedback (testing) and make adjustments to your sales process as needed

Get people ready to 'jump' on any early bird offers you might have, or special deals for the first 'x' number of sign ups.

What to do:

Keep it simple, and casual. This doesn't mean don't have a plan, but you certainly don't need to get fancy when it comes to an effective pre-launch. As we've said, the main purpose is simply to let people know that your offering is coming. I've found it works very well to do exactly that! For example, you might post something like the following on social media, and then send out a longer version over email.

"Big announcement! I'm so excited to share that my new program, the 'Get Published Book Bootcamp' for female entrepreneurs who want to bring their message to the world as an author, is going to open for registrations next week! I'll be sharing the exact strategies and 'must-knows' that I've figured out to create success as a best-selling author on Amazon. If you have a book inside of you that needs to come out, or you want to boost your brand and your traffic as well as expert status by being a published author, this is the program for you!"

Can you see how simple that is? You're not asking people to buy anything, you're just letting them know about something that is coming that would be of interest to them. And you're planting it in their heads as well. Here are some other things you could do or mention in similar statements:

List out what you are planning to include, and ask if there's anything else people would like to see.

Send out a mini-survey, i.e. "Assuming you would like to have a book, what's the #1 thing that has stopped you writing and publishing your book so far?"

Let people know exactly when the doors will open for registrations and if there will be a special time-limited discount offer or a bonus for the first 'x' amount of people. I strongly recommend you include these sort of offers (one or the other usually) in your launch process. Never assume people will buy your thing even if they want it - they'll often 'think about it', which means 'forget about it'! When you create an urgency-based incentive to buy now, everybody wins - remember that your product or offering is there to help people, after all!

Show 'sneak peeks' of content or even a look at the visuals of how your program will work.

Run a free webinar or teleclass, teaching valuable content on a topic that is part of your product or offering, or directly related. This builds interest in you and what you do, allows you to 'give back and add value' to your community at the same time as serving directly as a lead-in to your sales process. The way it would work is that at the end of your webinar or teleclass - or even throughout it - you would make mention of your upcoming offering, and how it can help the listener/viewer. Remember to keep it simple! For example - "If you've enjoyed and benefitted from this free teleclass on ______, I know you will just LOVE my upcoming ____________! What it covers is ________, and it's designed exactly for ____________! Here are the details:

Create a free opt in for people to access, such as a 3-part audio or video program teaching useful and related content, after which the 'doors open' and/or people receive an invitation to buy. This could also be done with 3 emails followed by an invitation to buy. (Of course it doesn't have to be exactly 3, but it's widely accepted as the ideal number for this sort of sales funnel, with the 4th communication then being the sale offer.

See if you can line up some guest posts and/or interviews on other blogs, to go live on the day or week of your launch. Typically the way this would work is that you provide great free content relevant to the readership of that business owner, and then at the end a mention is made of your brand new product or offering and any special promotion you might offer just for those readers/listeners.

Launch

Your launch period is the actual frame of time in which the doors to your program or offering are open - namely in which people can buy your thing! It is super important to be prepared for this. A well prepared launch can mean the difference between a raging success and a complete flop.

Here's what you need to know to be prepared:

Firstly, is everything ready to go for your launch? This would include but perhaps not be limited to:

Sales page with purchase buttons connected to PayPal or your checkout provider of choice.

Option for instalment plan payment if the product is over $100 in value.

Redirect page - this means the page on your site that people are taken to after their payment is processed. I like to use a 'congratulations' page welcoming them to the program and also reminding them to look out for the official welcome email, and to check spam or trash if they don't see it.

Welcome email connected through Aweber / MailChimp / Infusionsoft - so that when people sign up they automatically receive a welcome email with everything they need to know.

Any affiliates or friends who will be helping you promote know that this is the day and have been given suggestions of email and social media promotions they can use.

Blog post announcement written and ready to push 'send'.

Sales email announcement written and ready to push 'send' on. Note that you can combine a blog post/sales email into one and the same - if you can write these with an element of education, entertainment and/or inspiration and not just 'selling' your results will sky-rocket!

TEST everything - go through the entire sales process yourself and make sure everything is working! Imagine how distraught you will be if your offering goes live and the sales buttons for some reason don't work!

Re-read and edit everything with a fresh eye- ideally have someone else do so as well.

Here are some things you don't necessarily need pre-prepared in order to go live with your launch. (Note that I don't really recommend pre-creating your entire product or offering before you sell it. If it does NOT sell you've wasted a lot of time, effort and possibly money on something that nobody bought and that needs either canning or redoing completely or at the very least 'tweaking'):

Offering or product fully created (I do recommend you have a draft complete!).

Note that if what you are selling is something for instant download, such as an eBook, then obviously it WILL need to be created before it's sold, unless you choose to do a pre-sale, meaning that your sale goes live with a discount offer and the proviso that the download will be received on 'x' date in the future. If you take this approach be damn sure that your offering then goes out to pre-buyers when you said it would!

Membership site completely set up - I recommend you have a draft or a plan for this as well and you could have the domain name purchased (mind you, you can also host your product or even a full program on your main site, it doesn't need its own site; that's kind of a 'nice to have' sort of thing).

All of the sales emails and promotions for the entire launch period pre-written: again, you COULD do this but it's not essential. Personally I like to create these sort of things on the fly and as-needed for Round 1 of everything I do, and then when I 're-promote' that offering I can re-use or just tweak them. But I'll admit that this approach can be stressful and sometimes I think how nice it would be to do everything in advance!

Reminder! If you have taken the time and made the effort to do your pre-launch as suggested above then on the day you announce the doors are open, people are not only expecting your offering but eagerly awaiting it! That's exactly what you want. Don't get me wrong - if your offering is freaking awesome and exactly what your tribe most desires and need it will still garner a response with an 'out of the blue' launch, but you do risk people basically overlooking it simply due to a full inbox and a busy life. That aside, it's common sense to think that if people have already been anticipating something they are all the happier to see it has arrived.

On launch day itself, here is what needs to happen:

Sales email/blog post gets emailed out and promoted on social media.

Any affiliates or promoters send out their promotions (always check in with anyone who is supposed to be promoting for you, as they will possibly forget ... remember it's YOUR business, not theirs!)

Additional social media promotions posted.

In particular make sure any promotions (all promotions!) that are going out highlight any early bird or 'first x sign ups' offers you might have.

Check on sales! Don't be alarmed if your sales are quite low on day 1 of (for example) a 3-7 day promotion. It's normal for up to 90% of sales to come on the last day UNLESS you are offering a very strong incentive for the first 'x' sign ups; in that case most of your sales should come at the start.

As a side note to that: a typical launch/promo period should run maximum 3 weeks, with any early bird offers running for no more than 7 days. Many people find that a shorter 'special' promotion period, such as 48-72 hours, is most effective for this sort of thing.

Consider running a Facebook ad that goes only to existing likers in your community and straight to your sales page. Do NOT try to sell straight off Facebook to anyone who is not already a current liker, as your success rate will be dismal. Aside from any direct sales it may result in, the obvious benefit of a Facebook ad about your product is that it means what you are offering is constantly 'in people's faces', so they are thinking about it a lot and more likely to buy even at some future point.

Check that any guest posts/interviews have gone live and be

sure to thank the business owner.

Throughout the rest of the launch, here is what needs to happen:

Continue to work on/pad out your content. In particular make sure that your 'Week One' content is going to be ready.

Sales emails and social media promotions - social media might be daily, and you could highlight different things such as features or benefits, testimonials, why you created it, why it's unique and so on. Sales emails/blogs can be every few days apart however when you are in the final days and hours of your promotion period - such as an early bird period or if you have 'x' number of VIP spaces (for example) still left - then you can do them more often. Don't be afraid to send a LOT of emails when time is running out to get a special offer. If someone gets so upset at this that they unsubscribe then they were never truly part of your community anyway. The reason to send a lot is simple - people are busy, and easily distracted. They may see that your offer is down to its final day, and tell themselves they'll get it later that day but then they forget. If you truly want to run a successful launch and help those who you are meant to help then don't let them forget!

Is there anything you need to do to liaise with people who have already purchased? Do it. If your product is an instant download you may want to send a follow up email to see how people are finding it (gather some testimonials and get valuable feedback!) as well as to give some implementation tips.

I definitely recommend you run an additional free promotion such as a webinar or teleclass. Exactly the same approach as you did in the pre-launch, but this time you are directly promoting the sale. For both pre-launch and live launch online events like these I recommend that you record the event and send out the recordings with an enticing reason as to why people should listen to them. Most people who sign up for a free online class simply don't attend it.

Continue to follow up with any affiliates or promoters.

Follow up on any further guest posts or interviews with you that are going live, and thank the business owner.

Get super excited and be present on social media for the 'final countdown'.

Post-Launch

You may have noticed that all of the above advice was written under the assumption that your launch period will come to an end after a period of days or weeks. But what if you're selling something that is 'evergreen', meaning that once it goes on sale it stays available for purchase? If that's the case - for example if it's an eBook, self-guided or home-study program, or other instant download - I still recommend you employ the strategies I shared above when you first go live, as running it this way will absolutely increase your sales. If you just pop something out there for sale with zero sense of urgency or special promotion then people will respond with less than enthusiasm. Why should they, when you've told them (whether or not you said it verbally!) that there's no rush or need to take action now. So even if you are going to keep your offering on sale indefinitely then you absolutely should still run a launch promotion and fast-action taker/early bird offer. Now - on to 'post launch!'

Post-launch is the period of a week or so after your launch closes. Here's what you need to know and do in that time-frame:

Do a complete review and assessment. I recommend you make a list of everything that was covered during your pre-launch and launch, and basically note down what worked and didn't work, as well as anything to remember for future reference. The huge benefit of doing this is not just for the sake of the actual assessment but also because when you come to your next launch you will save so much time and hassle!

Improve any tech stuff that needs improving.

Same for any systems/communication i.e. what people receive/need after purchase.

Take down all promotions on your website - switch the sales page to draft if needed OR replace it (make sure you save the copy!) with a sign up box for people to get on the notification list for the next time.

Send Thank You notes to anyone who assisted in the launch.

Do a summary of the launch for your own sake, including a total of monies received.

Do something to celebrate your launch - even if it didn't go as planned I recommend you do this! Honour the time and energy you've put into this and reward yourself. You don't have to spend money to do this, but if you MADE money I definitely recommend that you let yourself spend a portion on yourself! I like to put aside 10% of all my earnings 'just for me'.

Take at least a day off ... or an afternoon if you can't bear to take a whole day off!

Well done on your launch!

Making money is not just about what you're selling!

Here's what you need to know about 'constant' marketing to build your brand and business.

The truth about running a successful business is that you are effectively always marketing. You might have heard the expression 'ABS' - Always Be Selling. Well, I guess this is true if you consider that even when you're not selling you ARE selling. You're selling you. Your brand. Trust. And connection. And how do you do that? Via effective marketing and communication! Now I'm no marketing graduate, so forgive me if I don't get the 'book definition' right, but here is what I consider to be 'must-do' marketing relevant to an online business:

Regular presence on social media (choose 1-2 platforms to do well, don't try and be everywhere).

Value based blog posts that are insanely shareable.

Images of you and your stuff frequently present on social media.

Links to your stuff seeded in to your blog posts.

Regular email communication: i.e. a weekly or fortnightly newsletter that goes out regardless of what promotions you might be running.

Effective customer service/communication in place.

Things work as they should (remember everything you do, whether done well or poorly, reflects on and therefore markets you and your brand).

Connecting/networking in relevant online groups.

Responding to comments/questions on social media.

Staying tuned in and listening to the conversation of your audience - paying attention to and responding to changes in your industry or in what your audience wants from you.

Here's the thing - when you think about how to best market yourself, you can make it as easy or as complex as you like.

You can study marketing and make big lists of everything you 'should' do to make it online, and maybe that's a good idea. Personally it's never how I've worked, and it sure hasn't hurt my business success or income growth. The way I like to think of it - and what has worked best for me - is simply to be me and be visible. Communicate daily in one form or another, whether a social media update, a blog, a newsletter or just be answering emails. Yes there are some things I schedule, such as having a newsletter, but even then it's loose scheduling - I don't stick to an exact day. Perhaps I should be more rigid with my communication and marketing efforts, but I've given up on trying. It doesn't suit my lifestyle or personality to be honest, and it starts to feel a little fake - something I'm sure comes across in my message.

The most powerful thing you can do in your marketing is to BE YOU. If you can do that all of the time, and weave in a mixture of education, inspiration and entertainment (or even one of those) in all that you do, you will be moving forward and making a difference as you also grow your community and list. Which is really what it's all about!

Before You Leave This Chapter!

I recommend you type out the checklists and ideas from this chapter that are relevant to you and your business. Do so now, so that when you next come to prepare a launch you are fully prepared!

Bonus exercise: write a half page or so in your journal of

how you'd like to feel about your own 'everyday' approach to marketing your business and building your brand.

CHAPTER NINE - SALES

Ah - sales - what evil people do to nice people, right? Except - wrong.

Probably the greatest thing I ever learned about sales was also the simplest thing I ever heard on the topic, and that was this:

Selling is love.

I know, right? MAJOR urge to eye-roll right now. But here's the thing. There's no point in you learning how to better sell yourself and/or your products and offerings (the selling of which IS, of course, selling you whether you like it or not) unless you are happy about selling. If you already are a total lover of all things selling, feel free to skip past to the bit where I share my practical strategies.

But if any part of you - or heck, every damn part of you! - wants to cringe, shy away and just feels plain ICKY at the idea of deliberate sales then you need stop. Reconsider. And choose to form a new viewpoint.

And here is where to start, with something I touched on a little earlier in this book -

The stuff you're selling; it's good stuff right? That program you're crafting, your consulting or coaching services, your eBooks, and all the many 'possibilities' and ideas that still exist only within your head? Is it true or not true that those offerings, once brought to life and to the world, will help people?

Hey - if it's not true or you're not so sure then I'll be the first to say don't sell them yet or possibly at all! This ain't about get rich quick schemes ... as if those things even work anyway ;)

So let's say it's true.

Let's say - gasp! - that everything you're creating and wanting to offer to your audience is high-value, based on their needs and desires and that you KNOW that if they absorb and implement what you're offering it will truly help to change their life in some way.

Let's say you know that your offerings are doing GOOD in the world, or going to.

Let's say you know that not just the individual products and offerings themselves are doing good, but that your whole MESSAGE is one of transformation and service, one that NEEDS to go out into the world and help people.

If that's the case, then how on earth can you think it's bad to sell your stuff to people?

Now, before you play devil's advocate and wonder if it wouldn't just be the right thing to do to give your stuff away for free, or at least to charge super low for it, let me squash that one right now -

Are you here to run a business, or a charity?

Do you want your business to be profitable, or broke?

Do you want to be able to reach more people and HELP more people, because your business is profitable and allows you the time, energy and reach to do that?

I absolutely DO believe in giving (a lot) of high value content away for free, or at a low price. Heck, look at what you paid for this book! I very well could have run it only as an online program instead, and charged hundreds of dollars for it, if not thousands. After all, if you implement everything I'm sharing with you in this book you stand to make thousands if not hundreds of thousands in return!

So no - I'm not saying that you SHOULDN'T create great, free, and low-cost content. Clearly we've already talked about that, and it's essential that you DO.

But your actual products, services and paid offerings?

People gotta pay for them! And it's going to be damn hard for them to do that if you don't deliberately SELL it to them.

So let me kill a few myths about effective selling right now -

'Build it and they will come' does not apply to online business, not for traffic and list growth nor for selling your stuff. That approach may have worked in the early days of blogging and online biz, but with god-knows-how-many-millions of new blogs being launched every week these days you need to actively make sure you stand out and are seen.

Selling (valuable) stuff does not make you a bad person. It makes you a person intent on changing people's lives, and on giving people something they need in exchange for fair compensation and something YOU need.

You will usually do people a disservice by giving high-value paid content away for free or at a low cost. People won't value it, won't implement it, and you have therefore helped them to move FURTHER away from their goals.

You do not have to be pushy, manipulative or 'salesy' (whatever that is!) in order to be good at selling.

You can sell very effectively from a place of love, compassion and genuine care, and that's what I'm going to show you.

How Effective Selling Works in the Online World ... or Any World

I've always had a bit of a natural gift for sales. And I'll admit it - I've always enjoyed selling. From the age of 4 or 5 I was selling my artwork and my Grandmother's citrus fruits door to door up and down my street. I was even savvy enough to realise that if I brought my 2-year old brother with me my sales increased due to the 'cuteness factor'. Throughout my childhood years I formed numerous clubs which I charged entry for and sometimes monthly membership, and then pretty much put all the members of the clubs to work selling baked and other goods door to door (don't worry I WAS sharing the club profits fairly!). I also ran a pretty good trade of selling my second-hand toys and the like in the school yard at the age of 7, until the teachers put a stop to it.

By the age of 11, I was an 'Avon Lady'; and by 16, I was selling Nutrimetics Cosmetics and making as much as a cool grand a week. Not bad considering I was still under Australia's legal age to work at the time!

From as young as I can remember I soaked up any books on personal development and effective business including, of course, effective selling. As an adult, I've been fortunate enough to attend numerous sales training conferences and events, some of which were paid for me by my former employer, and some of which I paid for myself. In 2013 I spent over 50 grand (yes that's over $50,000!) on sales and marketing coaching - and much of what I'm teaching you in this book is filtered down directly from what I learned through that period as well as all the learning which came before it.

So I guess you could say that when it comes to sales I have a pretty good handle on it. I'm by no means the 'best out there', and I'm sure there's still so much for me to learn, but from a strategy as well as simply an 'instinct' point of view, I get selling.

And here's what I want you to get about it. I've taken the best of what I've learned practically as well as internally about sales over the years and am sharing only those top tips and 'must knows' with you - the stuff that works AND leaves a good taste in your mouth.

Kat's Sales Process

The process of getting someone to buy what you have to offer is very simple, and it comes down to one thing -

Do you know what your customer wants and needs, and do they know that you can give it to them?

Let's assume that you've implemented what I've taught you about marketing and getting 'brand you' out there, and you're now at the point where you're actually having either a 1-to-1 conversation or else selling over email or a sales page. Here's what needs to happen:

1. The very first thing is always 'know your customer'

An entire book could be written about client profiling or 'niching' as it's known, but here's what it really comes down to: what is the greatest problem or issue your customer has right now, and what is the solution you can offer to help them?

2. The next thing is 'know their why'

You have to go deeper. It's not enough to know that your client is desperate to lose weight, or make money online, or transform their relationship, or beat stress, or finally be able to sleep well again. That's the surface stuff. It's 'nice to know' (okay, important to know), but sales - particularly soul-based selling - depends on understanding the underlying motivation of your client, otherwise known as their 'why'. So if you think about that big 'must have' goal of your client, what is the REASON they want to achieve that goal? Why is it truly important to them? Why is it really, REALLY important to them?

(Hint: a 'bonus' to this question would also be to go into more depth on what that goal is really about. I.e. describe the emotions, feelings, details, and everything you can that has to do with how your client will feel once they've reached their goal)

3. It's NOT about you and what you have to offer

It's so not about you gorgeous. Sure, your journey and story can inspire your customers and it is a part of your sales process. But don't spend your entire sales conversation (verbal or written) talking about your sh*t. You're there to talk about your customer's sh*t. So do so, yeah? Listen. People will do anything for someone who truly listens to and cares about them. Be that person. Be good enough to shut up and be that difference in another person's life.

4. How can you help them RIGHT NOW?

Maybe you can't click your fingers and have your customer lose 10kg instantly, or start making 10k a month online. But you can definitely help them in some way right now. What is that way, hmmm? What message of hope or how-to or inspiration can you give your client (as part of your sales process ... make the 'sell' itself value based!) that will help and even transform them?

5. Paint a picture of the life they could have

Don't be afraid to be honest with your customer about how your message or offering will impact their life. You've created something good, right? The whole idea being that people are going to achieve change as a result of it. Change that they would not otherwise have? If that's true, then freaking talk about it! Talk about how damn great their life could be once they learn from you, work with you, whatever it is.

And talk about what path they're on right now and how that might continue to impact them if they do NOT get your thing.

I'm not saying be mean and of course it's not as though if they don't get your thing their life will FAIL. But seriously - they are listening to you for a reason. They want to know there's a solution. If you have it, tell 'em! And remind them that there's a reason they want that solution. It's because they don't want to continue on the path they're on. Maybe they can figure it out without you. But also - they haven't yet. Why would that change?

6. Ask for permission to sell

You don't have to shove your stuff down people's throats.

You can be subtle, gentle, and gracious and still be a master sales queen. One way to do that is to ask. Simply ask - would you like to know more about how I can help you? If it's written, then do it this way - If you've enjoyed what we've spoken about so far/what you've learned from me so far then you're going to love my " enter name of your program here" offering. You can click here to learn more about it. Even in your sales copy, use wording that asks for permission. For example - 'I'd love to tell you about ...'

When you repeatedly create value for people they will be THRILLED to hear what you have to sell them. They'll want you to tell them about it! Imagine how great it would feel to ask your customer 'would you like to hear about how I can help you', and have them say YES!

7. Share about your product or offering from a NEEDS-BASED point of view

The details of your thing are important. But details, schmetails, really. Do I really care how your product or service is delivered? Does it matter if I receive audios or videos or worksheets (oh my!)? Do I care about the exact method of support offered? Okay, sure. I probably do care about all of that to an extent. But what I REALLY care about, and what will ultimately determine whether or not I buy is very simple -

Is your thing going to get me from A to B, with A being where I am right now (stuck, bad, awful, sad) and B being the place where I long to be (awesome, fantastic, my dream, I can't believe it!)

I couldn't give two hoots about the details if I don't also get the solution; the benefit. So by all means mention what the features of your thing are. But it's the benefits you're really selling.

8. Be deliberate about who this is for and not for - use 'takeaway selling' if needed

Your stuff is not for everyone. I mean sure, maybe everyone needs what you're selling. But YOUR stuff is not for everyone. It's for your customer. Who is that person again? And just as important - who are they NOT? Don't be afraid to say 'this is not for everyone', and list out who it's not for. This is actually a sales strategy and it's called 'takeaway selling'. But really what it's about is being upfront about who you can best help. If I'm not your client I don't want (or really need) your thing and you don't want me.

Be a master of your domain. You gotta have a domain to do that!

9. Don't be afraid to ask for the sale and to put people on the spot

Ask for permission to sell, by all means. But once you have it you then need to actually sell! Don't assume that people will go out of their way to find your tiny meek little hidden purchase link, or to track you down and ask if they can give you money. They will NOT. You have to tell people exactly what it is you have to offer them, and then you need to tell them to buy it. Just be flat out honest about it!

'If you want these results, then click the link now and buy my thing!'

Pretty much :)

People need to be told what to do next. So tell them. Or you will lose them.

10. Man up and face your customer's objections or concerns

But first, perhaps, you need to address any concern's your customer might have. Put yourself in their shoes. Are they worried they won't have time to implement what you're teaching? That they won't get results anyway? That they've already tried 'everything'? That you're a scam artist? That it will be too hard? That there is some special reason it won't work for THEM?

List out the concerns your customer has. And address them, honestly. This can be your 'FAQ' section.

11. Reinforce the smart decision of your customer

Once your customer has purchased from you, it's your job to reaffirm that sale to them! Do this whether or not they're receiving instant delivery of their item. Ever heard of buyer's remorse? Make sure your customers don't get it. Send them extra love and value. Even in your order confirmation email (if you have one) you can congratulate them on their smart decision and reaffirm some of the awesomeness in store for them.

You want people to walk out of your sales process feeling excited, not scared and wondering what they've done!

Before You Leave This Chapter!

Here's the thing about sales -

It is as scary or as simple as you make it. If you tell yourself that selling is bad, that you're bad for doing it and that nobody wants your stuff and you'll probably never make money anyway, then all of that is true.

So why not tell yourself the opposite?

That selling is love, and that YOU are someone who sells from the heart, that you only sell to people who need your stuff and whose lives you can change.

And as for strategy, well, it works. The things I just shared with you form a simple but highly effective sales process; one that has literally made me close to half a million dollars in the past 12 months alone. But more important than strategy - even than my strategy! - is that when you're selling you are listening. You are being you. You are being understanding. And when all is said and done, all you're doing, really, is matching what you have with what your customer needs.

Give yourself permission now to take off the pressure around sales and to just go forth and DO it!

CHAPTER TEN – STAND OUT OR STEP DOWN

When I started blogging back in '07, it was relatively easy to make a name for myself. When I say 'easy', I mean that I put in 40 hours a week, largely unpaid, for several years. But during that time my list grew, and my income and I guess 'positioning' as a blogger (I wasn't really calling myself an online business owner yet) also grew; fairly organically in some ways.

40 hours a week for several years sounds like a lot, but I guess it's not considering that it was the foundation of a business that now makes high 5-figures a month. Would YOU put in 40 hours a week for the next few years if you knew for certain it would have that pay off?

I guess you would (or you probably wouldn't be reading

this) but before you do, there are 2 things you must know:

1. There is no way you have to wait as long as I did to start making money online!

2. There is no way in hell you'll really make it online unless you STAND OUT from what is now a very crowded marketplace.

I don't believe that persistence alone, and 'putting in the time' will lead to success. I'd like to think that it was my awesome writing and passion for what I do that allowed me the initial success I created in my online business, but whilst that's probably true to an extent, I would say that simply BEING THERE was also a big part of it.

Blogging was kinda new.

There weren't many people doing it, relatively speaking.

And certainly not in my niche at the time. I was the only trainer I could find doing that sort of stuff online. The idea seems laughable now!

So now, simply showing up and doing the work won't cut it. You need to be able to stand out. Heck, even I've had to learn to innovate and make sure I stand out - just because I was in many ways 'there first' doesn't mean my success is now automated. Competition is everywhere, and so here's the only way you really can win:

Don't compete. Don't even try. Because really, your goal here for your business success is to succeed at being YOU.

And since there is no other you out there, there's no need to compete. You're going to win every time. But also - you're going to lose every time you try to compete at against somebody who is not you.

So let's talk about how you can stand out and create a name and a brand for yourself; one that is based on the truth - no matter how cray-cray it maybe be! - of who you are.

Your Unique Entrepreneurs Advantage

You might have heard the term 'USP' (Unique Selling Point). I'm just trying to be different by making up my own phrases, but I love wording it this way instead - Unique Entrepreneurs Advantage (UEA).

It's kind of simple, really.

It's just about being you in full colour. Nobody wants a faded or photocopied version of you, yes? This means - speak as you really would speak. And live your life. For example, yesterday a potential client expressed concern that she wouldn't be able to really do phone coaching in her business as she can't rely on naptimes for her 1 and 3 year old and it wouldn't be professional if her clients heard them in the background.

I used to feel this way as well about my kids ... or cafe noise ... or about anything, really. I felt that I had to present a certain image or people would think badly of me. And you know what? It was really freaking stressful living that way. I was like a coiled spring, and I don't just mean when I was on the phone. I mean in general in my business - I felt a constant underlying fear of being 'found out'. Found out for what, you might wonder. And really it was a fear of being found out for being ME and living my life. Which is crazy!

Now, when I get on the phone with a client - potential or existing - I let them know that my kids are in the background and that they're young, and that they might hear them. Simple. Of course I don't do a lot of phone work and so I try to schedule it for when the kids are asleep, but it doesn't always work out that way and besides - kids sometimes wake up when they're sleeping!

That's just one example. And I can't tell you what a RELIEF it was to just be honest about how my life is. When I don't make a big deal about it, neither do my clients.

Do you see what I'm saying? Whether it's your kids, or your language, or your weird thought processes, or the things that get you fired up or ANYTHING - just be unashamedly you.

Here are some other questions to ask yourself to figure out what makes you unique as an entrepreneur. Answer them in writing, and in as much detail as you can:

What makes you so different to other people in your industry?
What are you so damn passionate about? (Doesn't have to be at all related to your business)

What are 5 weird things about you that nobody would guess?

What are 3 kind of embarrassing, but funny things about you?

In what way do you/your offerings go above and beyond?

What is totally unusual and unique about your business and offerings?

What 'truth' are you hiding from your audience because you think it would make you look unprofessional, or silly?

Start to think about how you can incorporate all of these things into how you do business, and remember that what it's really about is simple - be you!

Raving Fans

Truly being you is one of the most effective ways you can build your brand and shine as different from the rest. If you combine that with repeatedly delivering high-value services and offerings to your community (both free and paid) and you simply continue to do both you absolutely will succeed.

A raving fan is someone who will pretty much want to buy or download or attend every single thing you do - they don't even really care to look at what it is first! They just know that if it's from you, they want it. It's of far greater value to you to have a small list filled with true raving fans, than a big list filled with people who don't really care one way or the other about your message and just ended up on your list because they opted in at some point for some freebie.

So what separates a mildly interested/possibly disinterested list member from one who is a raving fan who wants all your stuff? YOU do. It's your job to cement the relationship once someone joins your list. You have to prove yourself to them and 'earn your keep' in their inbox.

Here are some ways you can take it a little further and make sure that those who come into your online community also become your raving and adoring fans.

Connect, connect, connect - you certainly don't have to do so daily, but you do need to connect OFTEN with your community. There are no rules as to how often. Some people do build a fantastic business based on daily email communication, and others only send emails or newsletters monthly. Personally I think somewhere in the middle is about right for most of us. At times I think I might start sending daily emails or lessons on 'living your dream life' as I feel I've got so much to say that is important! But then I know myself well enough to know that if I did commit to doing that I wouldn't keep doing it.

What has worked very well for me is a regular weekly email newsletter summarising my latest blog posts, any special offers for my subscribers and general 'hello' and news from Kat. In addition to that I would send extra emails if there is something special I want people to know about - such as a free webinar - or of course if I'm running a launch. I also connect daily on my preferred social media outlet, which is currently Facebook. One thing to remember with figuring out how much YOU should connect is that it needs to be enough to build that relationship, but not so much that the bulk of your available work time is spent connecting and you have no time left over for creation!

Never forget that you are here to run a business, and businesses need to make money. Something I do quickly at the start of each day, just as an aside but relevant to this, is to ask myself "What do I need to do today for income purposes?" It's a simple check in to make sure your profit-based activities don't get left until last (usually meaning not done!) while you spend the day on email and social media.

Be a superhero. If you want to stand out and be remembered by those in your audience then do something different and (in the eyes of your community) fantastic. For example, give away some of your best stuff for free. I don't mean give away your actual paid programs, but what if you ran a webinar in which you actually taught your real system instead of just touching on one or two useful points? Most free webinars and trainings are full of quite a bit of fluff, and I know I've been guilty of that at times as well. But one of the most effective free trainings I've created - one that resulted in a lot of leads and paid business for me - was when I ran a webinar called '5k in 7 days' and I taught the exact system I use to make money - every part of it. (You can search that training and my name if you want it!).

Now if you think about it, it's obviously impossible for me to cover in a one hour webinar what I actually teach in my full 8-week mastermind but I can still cover the STEPS, and that's what I did. And people so appreciated the value of that. It was definitely a superhero move!

Listen, listen, listen. To stand out and be unique as an entrepreneur; something you can easily do that is different to what most business owners do is actually pay attention to your audience! I find that many of us start out wanting to communicate with and listen to our followers as much as possible, and are excited to receive emails from them, and then as business becomes busier we forget to maintain that one to one communication, focusing instead on ways to reach more people as a group and sell our stuff. Never forget that your business is made up of individuals. People. Who have desires, needs, struggles and wishes. Every day, ask yourself -

How can I help?

How can I be of service?

What do people want and need?

When you stop listening you will, sooner or later - no matter how 'in tune' you think you are - become disconnected. You'll no longer know exactly what your audience most wants and needs, and that disconnect will be reflected in your communication and your sales and marketing processes. Ultimately, if you continue down that path, you'll end up just another bland and boring business and you certainly won't find many true raving fans on your list!

A simple way to listen in is to actually ASK - create a simple survey, encourage people to comment on your posts or to reply to your emails. Treat your customers like people you are in a relationship with - there has to be constant give and take for it to work, and if one party stops paying attention the relationship is going to suffer!

Never, ever, ever give up. The final - or perhaps first - and definitely most important step in succeeding and standing out in your business is the simplest, as well as, at times the toughest. And that is this -

You must never, ever, ever quit.

If you truly want to create your dream business and live a life on your terms then you commit to that dream and you commit to doing what it takes to achieve it. The vision might change along the way, but so long as you keep putting one foot in front of the other, regardless of the challenges you have to face along the way, you WILL get there.

Before You Leave This Chapter!

What is your biggest takeaway from this chapter? What tip would, once implemented, make the greatest difference in your business and ultimately in your life?

CHAPTER ELEVEN – MOTIVATION, ACCOUNTABILITY, AND ALL THE (NOT SO) LITTLE THINGS

If you've read and absorbed even 50% of what I've covered in this book you are now fully equipped from a strategy and also a mindset point of view to go out and create your own multiple 6-figure business, doing what you love. Or to grow the business you're currently in. The truth is that any of us are capable of creating business success if we make up our minds that we will. Strategy and 'how-to' is certainly of benefit, and for that reason I've openly shared with you the exact systems and tools I use in my own business as well as with my clients. But even without all of that, you STILL have what it takes.

You always did and you always will. There's nothing that

anybody else can teach you to outweigh what you already have within you.

Before I bring this book to a close, I would like to share just a little of what I do in my business and life to stay motivated, accountable, and on track. These are all the little or perhaps not so little things you need to know about creating a business that you not only love but also one that serves you and your lifestyle; such that you truly are 'living your dream'.

Time and money are two of the most precious commodities you have. If you learn to use them both wisely you will reap many times over the value in return. Here are a few thoughts on making time work for you:

Time - if you have a life outside of your business, or want to, then a smart approach is to decide in advance how much time you are willing to put in each day. It's fine to go outside those boundaries, but having boundaries in the first place means you'll knuckle down and work 'smart' when you are working. Be reasonable about how much time you need to invest to grow your business but also how much you need leftover for your family, yourself, and other areas of your life. It's worth assigning yourself a work 'roster' so you know in advance what your week looks like. If you break it, that's fine - but having it there will serve the purpose of keeping you more easily on track.

Consistency - in terms of how much time or effort you should put in, your greatest results will come about when you're consistent. Anything that you give attention to on a daily or near daily basis is something that you will improve at, and get results in. It's far easier to commit to doing something for, say, 2 hours a day, 6 days a week then telling yourself you'll do one big block of 12 hours or even 2 smaller blocks of 6 hours each. Have a work routine that works for you - change it as and when needed, but avoid just making it up as you go along. For the vast majority of people that method really doesn't work.

Effort - commit to showing up and doing good quality work in your business. If you're going to invest the time then make it worthwhile, yes? This means, go into your work day with a clear action plan for your important priority tasks that must be done that day and do them FIRST. For example, today my top 3 are:

1. Write for an hour (which is always my daily #1)

2. Put together and send out my weekly newsletter

3. Prepare slides for the free webinar I'm running tonight

I know that once I've accomplished those 3 things I can rest easy for the rest of my workday, and turn my attention to social media, email and all the little things. The reality is that I've had to discipline myself to be able to let go of the need to get everything done, and learn that it's just not possible. So my list of little things actually consists of quite a few not so little at all things and I usually end the day with that list still seeming endlessly full. But here's what it comes down to: if I focus my effort on the little things, the things that pull at me and scream they 'must be done', I run out of time for the tasks which will help me reach my true business and life goals. Learn to put first things first and to just 'get over' the need to complete everything else.

Know your why -Being in business for yourself is certainly one of the most empowering and exhilarating things to ever experience, in my mind. But it's also one of the toughest, and absolutely not for the faint of heart. If you're going to be able to get up day after day and do what you need to do, even when you don't feel like it, even when it means saying 'no' to other things that could demand your time and attention, even when you're not yet making money, even when your great ideas flop and fail - you need to have a will of iron and the discipline of a soldier. And even those things alone are not enough.

What you really need, and what will actually dictate your motivation and whether or not you're able to follow through and keep putting one foot in front of the other is whether or not you know your deep and burning 'why' for your business. If you're still not sure of that, do some journaling TODAY to figure it out -

Why do you really want this? Why is it really, REALLY important to you? Why are you willing to keep on keeping on regardless of what you have to face along the way, and what makes you certain that no matter WHAT you will never, ever, ever quit?

Find your why and you find motivation for life, even during

the toughest of times.

Get the right support - It's a lonely business, being in business for yourself. It doesn't matter who you have in your corner, nobody is going to care about your business as much as you do! Which is fine, but it's not to say that you shouldn't make an effort to surround yourself with a support crew of friends, mentors, fellow entrepreneurs, coaches, and staff/people on your team. You don't have to bear the whole load alone, and nor should you. Here are my thoughts on finding the right support:

Staff/team members: outsource early, and often. When I first brought a customer service assistant on board I felt that there was no way I could afford to do so. But I knew that I was drowning in emails and that that in turn was costing me time on creative projects and therefore money. It's normal to feel you can't afford staff or paid support when in fact you MUST find a way to do so. You absolutely should do your research and not just throw all your profit away on staff, but if you need to stretch things a little bit to pay someone to do the stuff you're not great at doing or don't WANT to be doing so that you can get back to creating stuff that makes money ... well. Do so.

Personally I have a mixture of long term staff and occasional casual support. I've built my team gradually, as and when I need to, starting with my first assistant once my business was making a few grand a month. Some people wait longer but I really do think it holds you back. You don't need a whole team but you also cannot yourself BE a whole team, or at least not if you value your sanity and having any free time!

Use motivational and accountability strategies to keep you on track -

Some of my favourite are:

Vision boarding: I use Microsoft Word to create an image and word based vision board of what I'm wanting to create in my business and life. It's a bit of time to create (I do it maybe every 6 months) but it is SO empowering and inspiring to see every time I turn on my computer! I think it's crucial for us entrepreneurs to surround ourselves with things that will inspire and uplift us, and vision boarding is one of my favourite things for this. I like to use my vision board as my laptop desktop background - you may prefer to make a 'real life' one and stick it on your wall.

Tracking: tracking can be a little tedious but it can also be exciting. Even when it's NOT exciting - i.e. when you aren't reaching your goals in different areas - it's certainly important. It's pretty hard to hit your goals in different areas within your business if you don't measure your progress! Here are some of the things I track (and set goals to work towards):

- Income
- Profit (very different to income, as any business owner will know!)

- List growth
- Personal savings
- Conversion rate of new visitors to my site

'Fun' spending account: A year or two back I realised that I wasn't really giving myself permission to spend any money on myself 'just for fun', and anytime I DID want to buy myself something I felt guilty about doing so and/or didn't seem to have any spare money for it. So I decided to set up an online bank account to which I'd transfer just $20 a week automatically. As the year went on, I kind of forgot about it and then early this year I saw a stunning bikini that I would have loved. Straight away I thought 'well that would be a waste of money and besides, I don't really have any spare funds this week for a $150 bikini!' And then it hit me - my 'fun spending' account. I'd forgotten all about it! I logged in and sure enough had more than enough there for a bikini - in fact I had $842 sitting there! It was a fantastic feeling. Why not open some accounts yourself for various things, and transfer $20 or so a week to each? It's an easy way to build savings towards a particular goal and it also sends a message to the Universe that you are serious about having that goal achieved. Some other accounts I have, which I fully believed have played a key part in my achieving my dreams in the related areas, are:

- Dream Home and Office Account
- Designer Handbag Account

- First Class Business Coach Account
- Tithing Account
- Giving Account
- An account for each of my children

Be, do, have dreams: one of my favourite and most transformative exercises to do is called my 'be, do haves'. It's such a simple and yet such a transformative exercise to do! All you need is pen and paper, or a new computer file, and a timer. Set a timer for 3 minutes and then just start flat out writing down everything you would love to 'be' in your life over the next 6 months. Do another 3 minutes for everything you'd love to DO and a final 3 minutes for everything you'd love to HAVE. Don't be afraid to dream bigger than big when you do this exercise! Why not ask for what you really want? Heck, even if you don't quite make it you'll end up a lot closer than if you don't set it as a goal at all! Some of the things I have achieved in my life which I first set as 'be, do, have' goals (and in some cases had on my dream list for YEARS) include:

- Finishing and publishing my first book
- Becoming a best-selling author
- Creating a program that helps people to figure out what they really want from life and then make it happen

- Finding a great editor for my books

- Finding a great cover designer (these last 2 items were in some ways harder to achieve than actually writing the books in the first place was!)

- Getting abs back after having a baby ... and then again the second time!

- Packing up all our possessions and officially becoming residents of the world, living the laptop lifestyle and making all of our money online

- Paying off credit card debt

- And much, much, MUCH more!

I highly recommend that you take 10 (actually 9!) minutes right now to do the 'be, do have' exercise, and then why not diarise a note to yourself to repeat it every few months. Something that works really well, by the way, is to create your vision board based on these be, do have goals.

Average of 5

You may have heard the saying that you are the average of the 5 people you spend most of your time with, and I believe this to be very true. So what that means is if the people you spend your time with are dragging you down or even simply not lifting you up, it can be tougher for you to achieve success, your dream biz, and dream life as fast as you might if you were surrounded by support, encouragement, and also by the inspiration and proof that your dreams are possible.

When I first heard of this concept I was a little concerned as at the time I spent most of my time with a baby and my husband (who used to be very sceptical about this whole 'create your dream biz and life' thing!) and the occasional catch-up with a friend. I really didn't feel that I had any regular input from other women who dreamed big like I do, and could support me and perhaps even lift me up to a higher level. Many women I speak to feel exactly the same way, and wonder if they should 'sack' their friends and find new ones. While it's actually quite common to move on from old friendships as you move more and more into being a woman entrepreneur, it's not actually essential to sack friends or your partner or kids. :)

Here are some ideas that anyone can put to use right away to create a powerful environment of inspiration and support:

- Get a mentor or a coach.
- Join a mastermind of some kind that includes forum access where you get to regularly engage with other like-minded women.
- Go out there and create your own success network. If you are feeling alone and stuck I guarantee you're not the only one who feels that way! Ask around and see if anybody would like to join you in an

informal mastermind group where you can support each other and keep one another accountable.

Who can you share your successes with? If you do belong to any networks or masterminds, don't be afraid to share your successes as well as your challenges. Don't assume people will encourage or cheerlead you off their own bat - sometimes they will but honestly you CAN just ask!

And my final advice on motivation and accountability is this -

Don't be afraid to want to be a true and super brightly shining star. Aim for the heavens, and if you reach the clouds then how cool is that?! I remember a few years back my business mentor asked me what my money goal for a year from that time was. I told her that maybe I was being naive but I honestly thought I could achieve 2 or even 3 million dollars in gross business revenue. At the time my gross was around 350-400k. Her answer to me was simple -

"Well if you aim for 3 million, and you hit 2 - I guess everyone's going to be happy!"

I don't know about you, but I'd rather dream bigger than big every time, and if I don't quite hit it so be it - I know I'll end up a lot further along than if I try to play it safe or be (dreaded word!) 'realistic'!

Before You Leave This Book!

You were born to shine so damn bright. Give yourself permission NOW to say yes to creating the business and life you really want and start taking daily practical action as well as 'inner' action using the strategies outlined in this chapter.

Right now, I have no idea or way of knowing where you are in your business journey. But here is what I do know -

You can do this.

You have everything it takes, and then some.

You were born to succeed, and not just on the world's terms but on YOUR terms. You have it within you - right now - to create everything you desire for your business, for your life, for yourself.

So what are you waiting for gorgeous? Stop trying to figure it out in advance. You don't need to know the how. You don't need to have the time, the money, the anything. All you need to do is take a deep breath, close your eyes, run as fast as you can, and jump.

And I PROMISE you that you will fly.

Remember -

Life is Now. Press Play.

Kat x

EXTRACT FROM - THINK LIKE A RICH CHICK! GET MOTIVATED, ENERGISED, AND FALL BACK IN LOVE WITH LIFE!

Chapter One - Where True Energy is Found

Do you remember a time when you couldn't wait to jump out of bed in the morning, so in love were you with what was in store for you?

Do you remember feeling so damn happy that you get to be you, that you get to live your life?

Do you remember ever feeling just incredibly blessed to have so much opportunity all around you, and to know that life has so much good to offer you?

Perhaps you can right away think back to the last time in your life when you did feel these things. Perhaps you're lucky enough to be living it right now, and as you read the above questions you're smiling and thinking 'Yep! That's me!'

Or perhaps you're saddened to realise that no, actually; you can't remember when you last felt that way. Or that you can only vaguely recall such a time, and it seems so long ago and almost impossible to really imagine as having been part of your life.

Regardless of what your current reality is, I'm here to tell you that you deserve to live a life that makes you want to catapult yourself out of bed each morning. You deserve to feel certain you are doing what you're meant to do and you deserve to feel good - no GREAT - whilst doing it.

You deserve to love your life; to be in love with every part of it.

And you deserve all of that now.

If right now you're experiencing anything LESS than that, you're not alone. And it's not your fault. But it's also not how you have to continue, not for another week, another day or even another moment.

As of right now, I give you permission to start living a life you adore.

I give you permission to feel fabulous about being you.

I give you permission to feel excited again! Energised! And lit up from within.

And I give you permission to achieve all that you want to achieve and also enjoy the journey.

So here's what we're going to do.

This book is all about how to reclaim your MOJO, lady. It's about decluttering your soul of that heavy weight and constant sense of overwhelm, neverendingness and repetitiveness or even despair. And it's about filling you up from within with energy, vitality, vibrancy, joy, certainty, and love.

It's about turning you into someone who visibly shines their light into the world. Whose positive presence can be felt. Who knows that they are on path, even when at times things get tough or just plain suck.

The truth is that you don't have to spend another moment feeling anything less than thrilled and joyous to be you. Maybe it sounds a little over the top; maybe you even want to roll your eyes at the idea that things could be that good, but here's the thing -

There is no reward lying in wait for those who suffer for their dreams.

And it's really not the way you have to go about creating them.

So if it's you who gets to choose - and you do - then

wouldn't you rather choose to feel amazing? And doesn't it make sense that if you COULD harness that feeling on a daily basis and start to really shine at being you that you'd probably achieve everything you're striving for faster? But even if you're not so sure about whether or not that's true -

Aren't you just tired of life feeling like such hard work?

I'll let you in on a little secret. It's kind of the premise of this entire book. True energy, true 'va-va-voom' and mojo is found when you start letting yourself be who you really want to be and who you're truly meant to be. It's found when you give yourself permission to live with purpose. From a place of passion and flow. It's found when you take the time to tune in to your values, and what's really important to you.

So before we go any further, let's make a pact of sorts -

Let's agree that you're going to be open to having things work for you on your terms.

Let's agree to being open to being 'allowed' to do what you love, whether in business or in life.

Let's agree to being open to it being effortless, even easy.

Let's agree to being open to it being fun!

Let's agree that you don't HAVE to suffer to succeed.

And let's agree that you can start reclaiming your mojo and abso-freaking-lutely loving your life as of this very moment.

Here's to you beautiful - the world is at your feet and it's time for you to get out there and claim it on your terms!

To Do

Write a short list of 5 or 10 points, more if you feel the urge. Use this sentence as a guide, and simply fill in the blank at the end -

I give myself permission to ___________________________

I give myself permission to ___________________________

I give myself permission to ___________________________

I give myself permission to ___________________________

I give myself permission to ___________________________

I give myself permission to ___________________________

I give myself permission to ___________________________

I give myself permission to ___________________________

I give myself permission to ___________________________

I give myself permission to ___________________________

For more kickass books for kickass women, including free downloads go to:

www.booksforkickasswomen.com

MORE BOOKS FOR KICKASS WOMEN ENTREPRENEURS

REVOLUTIONARY FUCKING LEADER

1. Revolutionary Fucking Leaders: Quite Being So Vanilla. Unleash Greatness. Have It All.

2. Selfish Bitch: A Manifesto for Driven Woman Who Want It All, And Are Not Afraid To Take It

3. Purpose Passion Flow: Get Aligned. Speak Your Truth. Make Millions Being You!

4. The Anti-Marketing Blueprint: Getting Your Message Out When You Don't Fit the Box and Don't Give a Damn

5. Decide to WIN – Unleash Who You Are, and Go All In to Create the Life You Want! !

6. Flip Into Your OMG YES Life – How to Get Out of Your Own Way, Step the Fuck Up, and Let Money and Success Flow!

MAKE SHIT HAPPEN

1. How to Journal and Make Sh*t Happen! – The Book Every Women Craving an Exceptional Life Must Own!

2. Sprint Your Way Rich – The Adrenalin Lovin' Gals Guide to Self-Created Wealth Online

3. Act First, Think Later: The Kickass Entrepreneur's Guide to Rapid Success in Business and Life!

4. Launch It! – How to Create, Launch and Market Your Information Product in 2 Weeks or Less

5. The 25-Minute a Day Formula To Achieve Everything You Ever Wanted, in Business and Life, In 12 Months or Less!

6. Show Me Your Soul – There is a Magic Pill: You're Just Too Scared to Swallow it

RICH CHICKS GUIDE

1. The 100k a Month Formula: For Kickass Women Entrepreneurs Ready to Suck It Up and Finally Play BIG!

2. The Push: The Rich Chicks Guide to Being Mother-Freaking Exceptional, a Superwoman, the 1% and Okay With It

3. Rich Chick's Guide to Beating Overwhelm and Procrastination and Getting Sh*t DONE!: Productivity for Women Entrepreneurs Who Want It All, Now!

4. This Ain't No Dress Rehearsal Baby!: The Rich Chick Guide to Kicking Fear's Butt and JFDI'n it NOW!

5. The Rich Chicks Guide To Living a Fantasy Dream Life: Even When it Seems Impossible, You're Scared Shitless, or You're Not Even Sure What You Want!

THINK LIKE A RICH CHICK

1. Think Like a Rich Chick! And Live the Laptop Lifestyle, From Anywhere in the World: A Step-by-Step Guide to Creating Location Independence with an Online Business

2. Think Like a Rich Chick and Create your Millionaire Mindset

3. Think Like a Rich Chick! And Make Money Online!: The Step-By-Step Guide to Creating a Multiple 6-Figure Income, Dong What You Love!

4. Think Like a Rich Chick! Get Motivated, Energised and Fall Back in Love with Life!

5. Think Like a Rich Chick! Stop Working So Hard and Create The Life You Damn Well Want!

6. Think Like a Rich Chick! And Own Your Greatness – Quit Screwing Around, and Do What You Came Here to Do!

7. Think Like a Rich Chick and Find Your True Voice: It's Time to Press Play on the Business and Life You Were Born For!

STOP FUCKING AROUND

1. Stop F&*king Around, And Figure Out What You Want From Life!: the No BS Guide to Finding Your Purpose and Living with Passion and Flow!

2. It's Only Money, Honey!: Why Budgeting and Frugality Will Never Make You Rich, and the TRUE Fast Track to A Million-Dollar Biz

3. Hotter, Richer, Happier: The One Secret to Getting Everything You Want, and Living Your Dreams

4. Quit Fucking Around and Live Life on YOUR Terms – Success Mindset and Hardcore Strategy to Help You Take Immediate Action and Change Your Life, Now!

BADASS BUSINESS BABES

1. Harder, Faster, Bigger, Better – How to Do Business in the Fast Lane and Rule the WORLD!

2. Multi-Passionate Woman – Why It's Okay to Want AND Do It All, at Once if Not Sooner – And How to Make it Work!

3. Get Off Your Ass! – How to Find Your Ultimate Why, Create Like a Motherfucker, and Live Like You MEAN It, Now!

4. Unleash Your Revolution: The Rebel & Rule-Breakers Guide to Success, Leadership and Starting a MOVEMENT!

5. Making Money EASY! : Build a Business You Truly Adore, No BS, No Filter, No Excuse

SUPERWOMAN

1. Superwoman Success SMACKDOWN - 30 Days of Personal Transformation to Help You Succeed Beyond Your WILDEST Fantasies, and Live a Life You Love!

2. Rich, Famous, Free! : How to Have it All, Now. For the Driven Superwoman Who Just Won't Quit!

3. 100 Shit Hot Journaling Questions to Ask to Create Exceptional Success in Business and Life

4. Make Money Being You – The Driven Woman's Guide to Monetising Her Life!

ARTIST UNLEASHED

1. Powerful Fucking Creator Woman - For the Crazy Bithces Who Want To Change The World With Their True Art

2. The Zero Competition Formula – How to Unleash Your True Gift on the World and Make Your Mark By Branding You

3. Called – A Manifesto for Artists, Creators, Visionaries, Revolutionary Fucking Leaders Born to Change The World

4. Abundance – The Inner State of Rich, and How to Activate It, NOW

5. Hustle Bitch – Quit...... - Screwing Around, - The Bullshit, CREATE Your Dreams Now!

SHIT HOT RICH

1. Shit Hot Rich Bitch – For Driven Women Who Want to GTF Over Their BS and Finally Allow Success the Way They Were Born For.

2. Have It All! – For Rich Bitches Who Want The Business, The Body, The Life!

3. The Rich Bitch Guide to Taking Massive Action – For Driven Badass Women Ready to Get Their Shit Together, NOW!

4. How to Get Shit Hot Rich by Staying on Track to Your Dreams

For more kickass books for kickass women, including free downloads go to:

www.booksforkickasswomen.com

FREE BOOK FOR YOU!

Each month I give away one of my best-selling books as a free gift when you join my (also free!) online community of kickass women entrepreneurs!

Just go to www.katloterzo.com/freegift , opt-in, and download your copy instantly!

It would be my absolute honour and pleasure to have you in my community and give you the motivation, inspiration, education and *butt-kickin'* empowerment you need to get out there and create the business and life of your dreams!

I have to warn you though ... my style is somewhat out there. I'm not gonna hold back on saying what I think. I may very well call you on your sh*t ... often. And if I think you're limiting your ability to create what you WANT to create and CAN create then I'll be coming down on you like a ton of bricks. Loving bricks, but still.

You can get a bit more of an idea of how I can help you by checking out these popular posts:

You're A Delicate Flower With A Core Of Molten Steel

www.katloterzo.com/youre-delicate-flower-core-molten-steel/

On The Days When I Doubt Myself

www.katloterzo.com/on-the-days-when-i-doubt-myself/

Sit Your Ass Down And Do The Work

www.katloterzo.com/sit-ass-work/

Serious About Monetising Your Life And Being Known For Who You Are? Read

www.katloterzo.com/serious-monetising-life-known-read/

When You Feel Anxious, Scared, You're Freaking The Fuck Out And You Don't Know How To Move Forward … Do This

www.katloterzo.com/feel-anxious-scared-youre-freaking-fuck-dont-know-move-forward/

Flip Into Your OMG Yes Life

www.katloterzo.com/flip-omg-yes-life/

Ride The Flow Wave Gorgeous, You Were Made For Bliss

www.katloterzo.com/ride-flow-wave-gorgeous-made-bliss/

Fall In Love With Something, And Do It For Life

www.katloterzo.com/fall-love-something-life/

If You Say You Choose To Be Rich, And Famous, And Have It All, Why Don't You Just Act Like It?

www.katloterzo.com/say-choose-rich-famous-dont-just-act-like/

What If You Just Focused On Your Mission?

www.katloterzo.com/just-focused-mission/

It's Ok To Love It And Need To Leave It

www.katloterzo.com/okay-love-need-leave/

Visit www.katloterzo.com now to download your copy of one of my best-selling books free, and join the community!

HOW KAT CAN HELP YOU

The High Vibe Mastermind

The Mindset and Strategy of Crushing It Online: For Driven Creatives and Hustlers Who Just Want More

Where I (and my team) provide and support you *daily* with the mindset and the strategy of CRUSHING it online!

I made this for the DRIVEN creative and hustler who just wants more. More What? ALL OF IT! And who I made this for? *I made this for YOU!*

Do you want more money, more time, more freedom? Then what are you waiting for gorgeous?! Join my High Vibe Mastermind today and get ready to be FULLY committed to the mindset AND the strategy of making your every known potential and dream ... not to mention those you've not yet

DARED to own?

And when you sign up today on a *trial membership,* not only will you get full access to the awesome content in High Vibe, you'll also get immediate access to over $4,000 in Bonus Gifts! That's over $4,000 in Bonus Gifts with (wait for it) *NO* obligation to stay!

It's my risk free guarantee baby!

SO why would I do this?

Simple. Once you see the immense VALUE inside of The High Vibe Mastermind I just ***know*** you're gonna LOVE IT! Check it out NOW!

www.katloterzo.com/highvibefreegift

In the High Vibe Mastermind you'll get access to a ton of 'foundation' stuff that I've done for so many years now I forget at times that I once didn't know how. Stuff that I can now do in my eyes closed, or it's already fully one, or else my team now do it for me.

I've been making a list of ALL of this stuff, and creating or having my team create, trainings and simple to follow step-by-step guidelines on all of it for you. So that whether you're complete start up, or well advanced like me, anything that you need to know how to DO or pay somebody else to do is CLEARLY and precisely laid out for you. I'll also have tech and other support available to you from my team as well as me for ANY questions.

In The High Vibe Mastermind this stuff will include, but not be limited to:

- ALL tech stuff from start-up onwards
- Lead / landing pages stuff
- Funnel stuff
- Putting membership sites together
- Facebook ads and other forms of advertising
- Basic design
- Basic web development and set up
- What to put on your website
- Social media management
- Social media content curation
- How to hire staff
- What to do with them and how to manage them
- Plus ANYTHING else you need that I or my team can create for you!! For real!

And there's more as well!

The High Vibe Mastermind is about having it ALL. The more I thought about what to include in it to TEACH you the more my head started to want to implode, because I don't LIKE making 'trainings' that teach 'how', I like teaching you how to think and how to LIVE, and that's where MY results come from so why would I teach anything else!!

I think there is little to no point in my teaching you how to make MONEY or DO things in your business if I'm not also showing you every ELEMENT of who you need to be in order to actually be the person who can DO it, on repeat, and get the results.

So this means?

The simplest way for me to teach, mentor, inspire and GUIDE you is simply to take you along for the ride of EVERYTHING I do that works, and also share with you as I implement new habits and changes.

www.katloterzo.com/highvibefreegift

My High-Vibe Mastermind is a community where entrepreneurs, leaders, creators, VISIONARIES come together to get into purpose-driven alignment and flow, to bring their passions to life and to make BUCKETLOADS of money simply by owning their awesome -

And letting it out into the world.

It's a community where I'll be pulling back the curtain on EVERYTHING I do:

- In my business.

- My money.
- My mindset work and thinking.
- My LIFE.

To get results!!

Where I'll not only guide, support, motivated, educate and empower you daily with straight up knowledge and strategy you can apply NOW, but where I'll quite simply let you look at:

- What I'm doing -
- How I'm doing it -
- What's working -or not!

And then turn MY week by week biz and life elevation activities into week by week trainings for you to use and create from!

But most of all?

It's a community where you'll lay yourself on the line to do what it takes to create the life you want and were BORN for.

It's a community which is going to blow your MIND with content, value, quality, and simplicity of APPLICATION, for every single tiny AND big thing you need to know, think, understand or apply to rock your business and your life!

Long story short, and before we go any further? It's a community you need to get into NOW!!

www.katloterzo.com/highvibefreegift

The High Vibe Mastermind

The Mindset and Strategy of Crushing It Online: For Driven Creatives and Hustlers Who Just Want More

ABOUT THE AUTHOR, KAT LOTERZO

Kat Loterzo helps ***kickass entrepreneurs, artists, visionaries and #revolutionaryfuckingleaders*** design the business and life of their dreams. Her special gift is in inspiring, motivating and *empowering* women who already know they can HAVE it all to get out there and TAKE it all.

Kat is a **best-selling author and an internationally renowned speaker, entrepreneur and coach,** as well as the founder and creator of literally dozens of online products and programs. She built a multi-million dollar a year (and growing) business, initially by teaching women how to create the body of their dreams, before moving 'officially' into her current role as a business and life coach, working with other equally determined women to help them make their business and life dreams reality.

Kat lives with her two children (Alyssa and Nathan), and splits her time between the Gold Coast, Los Angeles and Dallas. She is obsessed with great coffee, great wifi, great wine and great training of the mind and body, as well as creating as much content as humanly possible on the topic of alignment and taking MASSIVE #asskickery and action.

Kat is also an expert in "No B.S" coaching and would love to help you create a business and life you love, completely on your terms!

Connect with Kat and download her free book of the month at www.katloterzo.com/freegift

Learn more about Kat at:

www.katloterzo.com/about/

Follow Kat on Facebook at:

www.facebook.com/lifeisnow.pressplay

Check out the **The High Vibe Mastermind** and how Kat can help you SHIFT your mindset, focus only on the things that matter and make more money, FASTER, in a way that suits you at:

www.katloterzo.com/jointhehighvibemastermind

YOUR HELP PLEASE!

Did you enjoy this book, find it helpful, or love how it kicked your ass?

I'd love it if you could take 2 minutes of your time to leave a review for this book on Amazon, even if you purchased it direct from my website and not from Amazon. Just search for this book and my name on your Amazon site.

Thank you so much!

And don't forget –

Life is Now. Press Play!

Kat x

Life is Now. Press Play.

Made in the USA
Monee, IL
23 September 2023

43264418R00105